CHOCOLATE, CHOCOLATE & MORE CHOCOLATE!

Elie Tarrab

Photography by Danya Weiner

imagine!

imagine!

An Imagine Book
Published by Charlesbridge
85 Main Street, Watertown, MA 02472
617-926-0329
www.charlesbridge.com

Created by Penn Publishing Ltd.
1 Yehuda Halevi Street, Tel Aviv, Israel 65135
www.penn.co.il

Editor-in-Chief: Rachel Penn
Edited by Ori Lenkinski
Photography by Danya Weiner
Styling by Deanna Linder
Design and layout by Ariane Rybski

Library of Congress Cataloging-in-Publication Data

Tarrab, Elie.
  Chocolate, chocolate & more chocolate! / Elie Tarrab ; photography by Danya Weiner.
     pages cm
  title: Chocolate, chocolate and more chocolate
  "An Imagine Book."
  Includes index.
  ISBN 978-1-62354-020-3
  1. Cooking (Chocolate) I. Weiner, Danya. II. Title. III. Title:
Chocolate, chocolate and more chocolate.
  TX767.C5T35 2014
  641.6'374--dc23
                        2013003908

2 4 6 8 10 9 7 5 3 1

Printed in China, September 2013

For information about custom editions, special sales, premium and corporate purchases,
please contact Charlesbridge Publishing at specialsales@charlesbridge.com

CONTENTS

INTRODUCTION 4

TOOLS 7

TECHNIQUES 10
- Melting and Tempering 10
- Ganâche 14
- Dragées 17
- Dipping and Enrobing 18
- Molding and Pralines 21
- Hollow Figurines 25

CHOCOLATE BARS & SHEETS 27

PRALINES, TRUFFLES & BONBONS 43

CHOCOLATE TREATS 69

CHOCOLATE DESSERTS 97

CHOCOLATE COOKIES & CAKES 121

METRIC EQUIVALENTS 142

INDEX 144

INTRODUCTION

Nothing says decadence like chocolate. One of the world's most mysterious and sought-after substances, chocolate can be wielded into endless awe-inspiring and mouth-watering forms. Enticing and rich, modern and timeless, chocolate is the ultimate ingredient for fun. Whether it's a slice of Chocolate Lava Cakes (page 133) or a bite-sized Orange Liqueur Pralines (page 50) that tickles your fancy, chocolate can brighten even the dullest day.

Chocolate, Chocolate & More Chocolate! offers the household chef a window into the world of professional chocolate-making. Join seasoned chocolatier Elie Tarrab in an exploration of chocolate's many faces and nationalities, from Amaretto Mousse Truffles (page 58) to White Chocolate & Green Tea Bars (page 36). The book opens with a brief introduction to commonly used chocolate techniques that will ensure that each recipe turns out delicious and beautiful. In over 80 recipes, Tarrab presents a whole new world of unforgettable homemade treats.

About the author

Elie Tarrab is a lover of all things chocolate. He has studied at the **Valrhona** gourmet chocolate manufacturer in the pastoral Rhône Valley in France. Elie's passion for chocolate dates back to his childhood in Haifa, Israel, where he tasted his first, unforgettable chocolate delicacies. In 2006 Elie opened a chocolate boutique in Tel Aviv called **Cardinal** where he makes pralines, bonbons, desserts, chocolate bars and other treats.

TOOLS

To prepare chocolate products, a number of tools are needed. Some of the tools are basic, while others are professional and will allow to achieve the best results. This is a list of the recommended tools.

Bench Scraper
Use a wide, machine-washable, stainless steel bench scraper suitable for working with food.

Bowls
I recommend working with plastic bowls because, unlike glass and metal, plastic isolates the chocolate from the room temperature.

I recommend using a round, flexible microwave-safe bowl with clean lines. Flexibility will ease the removal of excess chocolate from the bowl.

Dipping Forks
There are a variety of forks for dipping bonbons and other small products. Such forks have between 2 and 5 long, thin tines that allow the chocolate to drip easily. There are also spiral-shaped forks for truffles. I suggest choosing your fork based on the comfort of the handle and the strength of the tines. I recommend that you buy a three-tined fork, a two-tined fork and a truffle fork (see items (E), (F) and (G) on page 9).

Electric Mixer
Make sure your mixer has both a wire whisk and a paddle attachment. Both the attachments and the mixing bowl must be heat-resistant.

Fine Strainer
For straining chocolate and spices, I recommend a large, metal strainer with fine wires that can withstand pressure.

Piping Tubes
Piping tubes can be bought in a confectioner's store. They can also be made at home by cutting a hole in one end of a plastic bag. There are a variety of sizes and shapes of tips available to purchase. The most commonly used tips have serrated or round tips and ½-inch or ¾-inch openings.

Polycarbonate Molds

These are professional chocolate molds. They are unbreakable and available in many shapes such as: pralines, bars and dolls, to name but a few. You don't need to clean them between use and they can be stored in plastic wrap. You can occasionally clean them in warm water with a gentle soap, and then dry with cloth. After drying, rub the contours of the mold with a clean cloth until they are shiny.

Silicone Brush

These brushes are good for spreading chocolate, as they are easy to clean and do not create leftover chocolate bits.

Spatula

I recommend a flat spatula, although an angled spatula can be useful for certain tasks. The head should be made from slightly flexible, machine-washable stainless steel (see item (B) on page 9).

Spatula Scraper

I recommend using a silicone scraper that is fit for high temperatures. I like a scraper that has a removable head (easy for cleaning) and clean lines (see item (A) on page 9).

Thermometer

It is important to buy a digital thermometer that shows fractions of degrees, ranging from -60°F to 400°F. It should be water resistant. (See item (D) on page 9)

Do not buy a thermometer that measures temperature with lasers or infrared, as they only measure the surface temperature of the chocolate.

Wire Whisk

I prefer to use a whisk made of thick, stainless steel wires that are cast into the handle (see item (C) on page 9).

A　　B　　C　　D　　E　　F　　G

TECHNIQUES

➡ MELTING AND TEMPERING

In order to work correctly with chocolate, we must first understand the properties of cocoa butter and how to achieve the desired results when working with it.

Cocoa butter is a vegetable fat. Unlike other vegetable fats, cocoa butter does not turn into liquid at room temperature, but rather it has the ability to set in different shapes with different qualities. Cocoa butter can produce many textures in chocolate bars; from shiny and smooth to lumpy and brittle. Tempering is the key to creating the right texture.

Tempering chocolate is a process which includes the heat treatment of chocolate for a specific time and at a certain temperature to create consistently small cocoa butter crystals.

The tempering process is made up of three simple steps:

STEP 1: MELTING
Melting can be done in a variety of ways:

1. In the microwave: Heat in 30-second intervals, stirring the chocolate between intervals.

2. Using a bain-marie double boiler or creating your own 'double boiler': Place a bowl on top of a pot of hot water so that the water is touching the bottom of the bowl. Take care to keep the water separate from the chocolate.

3. In the oven: This is a slow, steady way to melt chocolate. Set the oven to 113°F -130°F. Leave the chocolate in a bowl in the oven for several hours, until it has completely melted.

I recommend using a plastic bowl for the top layer of the double boiler. Plastic, unlike metal, doesn't conduct or accumulate heat, and will therefore isolate the chocolate from the surrounding environment temperature.

STEP 2: SETTING
• There are several ways to complete this part of the process. The classic way is on a marble countertop or surface that can absorb the heat of the chocolate. Pour out 90% of the chocolate onto the surface, leaving 10% in the bowl. The remaining 10% will be used in step 3.

Opposite: Tempering (continued on page 12)

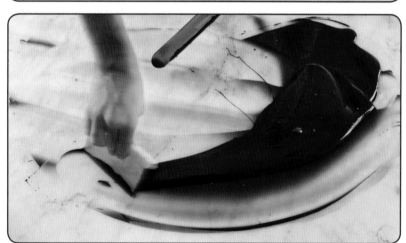

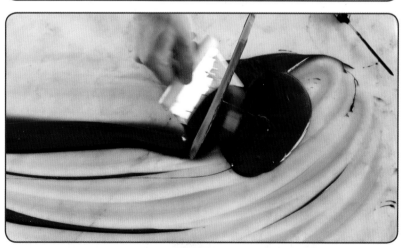

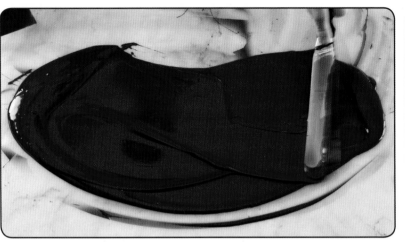

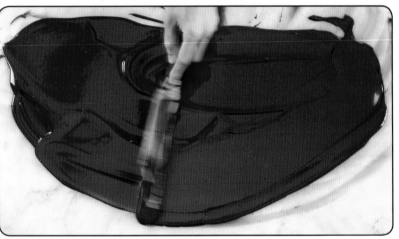

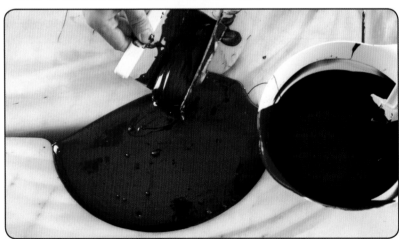
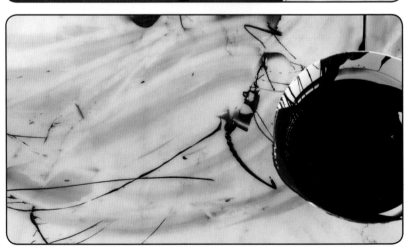

• The room temperature should be 65°F-70°F. Do not cool the countertop before this step.

• Spread the chocolate onto the surface, then gather the chocolate together. Repeat this step until dark chocolate cools to 82°F. Cool milk and white chocolate to 80F.

STEP 3: REHEATING
Return the chocolate from the countertop to the bowl, where the leftover 10% has been kept warm.

Maintaining tempered chocolate:
• It is very important to work at a temperature of 84°F to 90°F. If the temperature rises above 93°F, you will need to start from scratch.

• After the tempering process is complete, you will be able to work with the chocolate for a few minutes before it thickens. You may reheat the chocolate for a few seconds to make it more fluid, or add a bit of warm chocolate to thicken it. These steps can be taken a limited number of times before the chocolate becomes too thick to work with.

• Chocolate that has been contaminated with even a small amount of water will thicken into a dough-like substance. This can be used for baking or creams, but not for recipes that call for pure chocolate.

• Dark chocolate will set faster than white or milk chocolate.

• The more cocoa butter the chocolate contains, the more fluid it will be and the slower it will be to harden.

• The less cocoa butter the chocolate contains, the lower the required working temperature.

Recommended temperatures:

	STEP 1	STEP 2	STEP 3
Dark Chocolate	130°F	82°F	84°F - 90°F
Milk Chocolate	113°F	80°F	85°F - 88°F
White Chocolate	113°F	80°F	85°F - 88°F

Opposite: Tempering (continued from page 11)

➤ GANÂCHE

Ganâche is originally a French cream, most commonly known in its chocolate with cream form. Though ganâche is often made with a cream base, it can be prepared using chocolate and any liquid: such as water, milk, fruit puree or alcohol. As water and oil do not naturally mix, a technique is required to emulsify the chocolate and liquid. If this technique is done correctly, the emulsified chocolate and liquid will create a cream; one that is steady and strong, and won't separate back into its component parts.

The relationship between water and fats needs to be balanced correctly. If there is too large a quantity of fats, the ganâche will be heavy and lumpy. Thus, for every type of chocolate there is an appropriate ratio of liquid to solid. In addition, the texture of the ganâche must match the desired recipe. For example, bonbons require a firm ganâche, whereas a softer ganâche is needed for cake filling.

In most types of ganâche, we use corn syrup (glucose), inverted sugar syrup or honey to soften the ganâche and make it more elastic, while preventing the formation of lumps.

BASIC TECHNIQUE:
1. Melt the chocolate in a bowl. For the entire process the chocolate must be kept above 93°F so that the cocoa butter is completely melted; otherwise, it will separate from the cream.

2. Bring the liquids almost to a boil to create a 'semi-pasteurized' effect. When using alcohol, as long as the alcohol is at room temperature, there is no need to heat it.

3. Pour one quarter of the liquids into the chocolate and mix well, until a thick texture is achieved. Add in the rest of the liquids in equal stages, blending after each addition, until an elastic, shiny texture is achieved. At this stage it is best to use a handheld blender or electric mixer to blend the two components further, creating a finer emulsion. If the mixture is not shiny and completely smooth, add a small amount of liquids and blend again. Repeat this step until the desired texture is achieved.

4. Blending in butter can enhance the ganâche. As a final step, heat the ganâche to 93°F-100°F and add in butter at room temperature. The ganâche may be stored in a sealed container in the refrigerator for 2 weeks.

Opposite: Ganâche

▬ DRAGÉES

Dragée is a general name for any treat with a hard or crunchy center and a chocolate or candy coating.

In a professional kitchen, a mixing drum is commonly used for this process, but for home preparation, you can use a sturdy bowl instead.

First choose the hard center. For example, you can use dried fruits, such as figs or raisins, or nuts, such as almonds or hazelnuts.

The chocolate must be melted and warm. I recommend tempering the chocolate as described in Melting and Tempering on page 10, although this is optional.

This is a sample recipe for almond dragées:
1. Place the almonds in a bowl or on a countertop and sprinkle a small amount of chocolate on top to "dirty" the nuts. Mix the nuts and chocolate constantly, until the almonds are completely covered in a fine layer of chocolate. Continue to mix until the chocolate hardens, then separate the nuts from one another. Be careful not to use too much chocolate, as it will cause the nuts to stick together.

2. Once the chocolate is dry, repeat step 1 until the desired thickness of chocolate coating is achieved. I recommend cleaning the countertop or bowl between steps.

3. Once the final layer is complete, dust the almonds in cocoa powder, powdered sugar or a similar substance, and then sift away any excess coating material.

4. Store in a sealed container in a cool and dark place. Dragées may be stored in the refrigerator for 3-4 weeks; however, they should be served at room temperature.

Opposite: Dragées

► DIPPING AND ENROBING

The dipping technique, otherwise known as enrobing, is used to coat small items, such as bonbons, fresh or dried fruit and truffles in a fine layer of chocolate. Chocolate that is used for dipping has a high cocoa butter content, which makes the chocolate fluid. If, after you begin working, you find that your chocolate is not thin enough, add a small amount of cocoa butter as needed.

Bonbons are cream-filled French chocolates. The filling is usually ganâche.

This is a sample recipe for chocolate-covered bonbons:
1. This process requires a shallow frame, such as a 9-inch by 12-inch baking pan, where the chocolate will dry and set over the course of 24 hours. In the absence of an appropriate baking pan, construct a 10-inch by 13-inch baking pan using thick aluminum foil. Fold the edges of the foil to create walls. Line the bottom of the foil with plastic wrap. Pour a smooth layer of ganâche into the frame. Leave the ganâche in a cool dry room (at a temperature of about 70°F) for 24 hours.

2. Once the ganâche is set, pour a fine layer of chocolate on top. It's best if the chocolate is tempered, as described in Melting and Tempering on page 10. Allow the chocolate to set for 20 minutes. Flip the ganâche over so that the fine layer of chocolate is on the bottom.

3. Cut the ganâche into 1-inch cubes. Separate the cubes from one another and leave in a cool room for an additional 24 hours.

4. On the third day, enrobe the ganâche cubes. Temper the chocolate, as described in Melting and Tempering on page 10.

5. Dip the cubes, with the ganâche side down, in the bowl of melted chocolate. While dipping, tilt the bowl so that the chocolate is in a diagonal line with the bottom of the bowl. Using a special dipping fork, remove the cubes from the chocolate without touching the sides of the bowl, while creating a gentle up-down motion to shake off excess chocolate. Straighten the bowl, then tap the fork against the edge of the bowl to remove the rest of the excess chocolate from the ganâche. Slide the bottom of the fork against the edge of the bowl to release leftover chocolate. Remove the dipped cube from the fork and place on plastic wrap, parchment paper or silicone. If the chocolate creates a puddle around the ganâche, lift the cube and replace it in a clean spot.

6. Make sure to keep the chocolate thin and fluid throughout the entire preparation process, as it has a tendency to thicken. If the chocolate hardens, reheat

Opposite: Dipping and Enrobing
(continued on page 20)

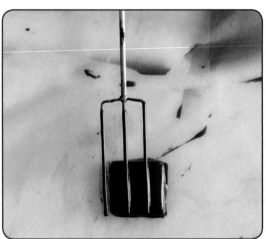
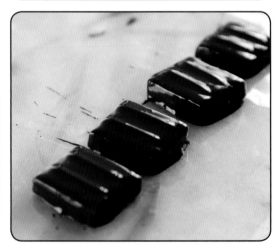

it and stir well. Do not heat above 93°F. If this problem occurs again, re-temper the chocolate.

7. Decorate the bonbons by lightly pressing the tines of the dipping fork into the top of each bonbon to create a design. Be sure to clean the fork after decorating each bonbon in order to ensure clean lines. Specialty baking shops carry tools that assist with the creative preparation of bonbons, such as a variety of dipping forks for truffles and bonbons.

▪ MOLDING AND PRALINES

The molding technique refers to any process in which chocolate is poured into a mold or form. Molding is employed in the Belgian method of preparing pralines.

Molding is similar to the enrobing process because you need to use chocolate with a high cocoa butter content. If necessary, you can enrich the chocolate with cocoa butter in order to achieve a thin and flowing texture.

Professional molds for chocolate are generally made of polycarbonate, and are therefore hard and unbreakable. The shine of the praline is partially dependent on the quality and upkeep of the mold. The mold must be washed with warm water and a gentle soap. Do not use sponges or tools as these will cause scratches in the mold. Dry the mold with a soft cloth, paying close attention to the indentations. Then use a clean cloth to polish the mold.

It is recommended to wrap the mold in plastic wrap before storing.

This is a sample recipe for cream-filled chocolate shells:
1. Temper the chocolate, as described in Melting and Tempering on page 10. Check that the chocolate hardens properly (in about 5 minutes). Chocolate that has been incorrectly tempered will not separate from the mold later in the process.

2. Fill the mold with the tempered, warm chocolate.

3. Tap the mold against the countertop to remove bubbles from the surface of the chocolate.

4. Flip the mold over the bowl, pouring out the chocolate, and tap on the back of the mold to help remove the chocolate. A fine layer of chocolate will coat the indentations of the mold. The thickness of the walls of the praline will be

Opposite: Dipping and Enrobing (continued from page 19)

determined by the texture of the chocolate and the physical force used to empty the mold. (Aim to leave a thin coating, $\frac{1}{20}$th of an inch in depth). Anything thinner than $\frac{1}{20}$th of an inch will be difficult to remove from the mold later on.

5. Once the chocolate has set slightly and lost its shine, scrape the top part of the mold, cleaning the surface of any excess chocolate, so that the mold is clean and the chocolate shells are ready to be filled.

6. Let the mold rest at 60°F for 4-5 hours or refrigerate for 15 minutes. Check that the chocolate has separated completely from the bottom of the mold.

7. Fill the shells with chocolate cream or another filling. The filling cannot be above 95°F; otherwise, it will melt the chocolate shells in the mold. Fill the shells, leaving $\frac{1}{20}$th of an inch empty at the top to allow you to close the mold with more chocolate. Let the filling set and dry for 24 hours in a cool room.

8. After one day, temper a new batch of chocolate and pour it over the shells. In order to achieve tight closure between the bottom and top of the praline, heat the top half of the mold slightly with a hair dryer before pouring the new chocolate on top. Scrape the top part of the mold, cleaning the surface of any excess chocolate. Once the chocolate has set, the praline is ready.

9. Flip the mold onto a clean surface. Lightly tap the mold to release the pralines.

Opposite: Molding

  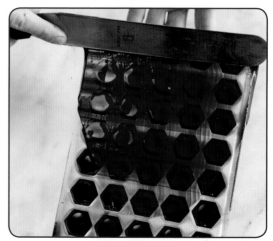

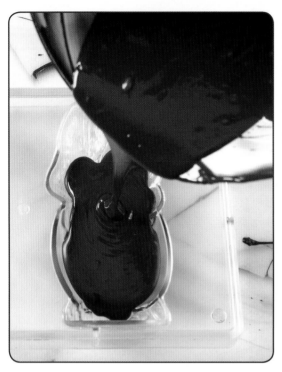

➤ HOLLOW FIGURINES

• There are many types of chocolate molds. For the most part, these molds are used to create flat shapes by pouring chocolate inside, removing bubbles and allowing the chocolate to set. There are, however, a variety of molds that can be used to create dolls or three-dimensional, hollow figurines. These molds always consist of two separate, connecting pieces.

• These figurines can be eggs, animals or other similar objects.

• To embellish these figurines with details, color specific points a different hue from that of the overall figure, using white chocolate or coloring.

• White chocolate can be dyed, using special coloring for cocoa butter. Most food coloring dissolves in water, and will therefore not dye white chocolate. In fact, these dyes will most likely ruin the chocolate.

This is a sample recipe for the preparation of a hollow doll:
1. Temper the chocolate, as described in Melting and Tempering on page 10. Fill 80% of one of the two pieces of your mold.

2. Immediately after filling the mold, close the second half onto the first and tightly shut the two pieces together. Check that the chocolate is spread throughout the entire mold. If not, tilt it in order to move the chocolate to the empty areas. Continue to turn for 4-5 minutes, or until the chocolate sets.

3. Leave the closed mold at 60°F, until the figurine separates from it. This will take 4-5 hours. Alternately, place it in the refrigerator for 15 minutes.

4. Gently extract the figurine from the mold, taking care not to break it.

Opposite: Hollow Figurines

CHOCOLATE BARS & SHEETS

- Peppermint Chocolate Bars 29
- Milk Chocolate & Nougat Bars 30
- Gianduja Bars 31
- Crushed Cocoa Bean Bars 32
- White Chocolate Caramel Bars 35
- White Chocolate & Green Tea Bars 36
- Rum Raisin & Hazelnut Chocolate Bars 38
- Black Tea Bars 39
- Milk Chocolate & Salted Butter Bars 41

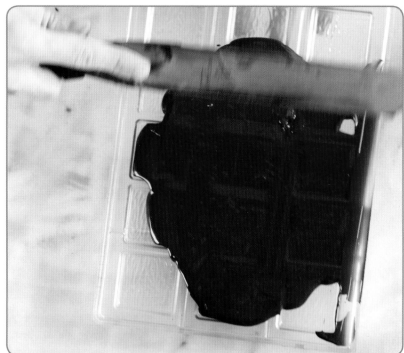

PEPPERMINT CHOCOLATE BARS

Makes

5

bars

One of the ways to enrich chocolate is with different essential oils. These can be purchased in health food and specialty stores in a variety of flavors, such as grapefruit, orange, lemon, lavender, mint and ginger. Be sure to purchase pure, high-quality oils.

Ingredients

17½ oz. dark chocolate (65-75% cocoa)
5-15 drops peppermint essential oil

Preparation

1 Melt and temper the chocolate, as described in Melting and Tempering on page 10.

2 Add the peppermint essential oil to the chocolate and mix well.

3 Once the chocolate mixture is ready, you can use it in one of two ways to create bars:

A Pour the chocolate into a chocolate bar mold. Tap the mold against the countertop to release air bubbles between the mold and the chocolate. Leave to set in a cool room for 2 hours. Remove chocolate from the mold and serve.

B Alternately, pour a thin layer of chocolate onto cellophane, parchment paper or silicone baking sheet. Allow to set for 1 hour in a cool room. Break and serve.

4 Pepperint Chocolate Bars may be stored in an airtight container, at room temperature or in the refrigerator for up to 3 months.

MILK CHOCOLATE & NOUGAT BARS

Makes

10

sheets

Nougat is likely to have originated in Italy in the 15th century. It has been a European favorite ever since.

Ingredients

NUT MIXTURE
½ cup almonds
½ cup hazelnuts
½ cup pistachios

NOUGAT
¾ cup honey
1 cup + 1½ tablespoons sugar
1 vanilla bean, split in half and seeds scraped
⅓ cup water
2 tablespoons egg whites
2 tablespoons cocoa butter

52½ oz. milk chocolate

Preparation

NUT MIXTURE

1   Heat the oven to 325°F. Roast the almonds and hazelnuts for 10-15 minutes.

2   Heat the pistachios in the microwave for 1-2 minutes. In a bowl, mix the nuts together and set aside to cool.

NOUGAT

3   Heat the honey with 1 cup of sugar, the vanilla bean and seeds and water over a medium flame. The honey may froth when heated, so it is best to use at least a one-quart pot.

4   When the honey mixture reaches 250°F, carefully remove the vanilla bean.

5   In a mixing bowl, beat the egg whites with the remaining sugar with an electric mixer.

6   When the honey mixture reaches 275°F, slowly pour into the egg whites. Continue to whip for 3-4 minutes.

7   Melt the cocoa butter and add to the mixture. The fats will cause the mixture to separate. As you whip the mixture, it will emulsify again.

8   Add the nut mixture to the nougat and mix well.

9   Transfer the mixture onto a lightly greased surface or parchment paper.

10 Cool for 2 hours and cut into cubes.

ASSEMBLY

11 Melt and temper the chocolate, as described in Melting and Tempering on page 10. Add the nougat cubes into the tempered chocolate and mix well.

12 Pour and flatten a thin layer of chocolate mixture onto parchment paper, silicone or cellophane. Allow the chocolate mixture to set for 1 hour in a cool room. Break into pieces and serve.

13 Milk Chocolate & Nougat Bars may be stored in an airtight container, at room temperature or in the refrigerator for up to 3 months.

GIANDUJA BARS

Makes

10

sheets

Gianduja is a European style of chocolate made with hazelnut praline. This chocolate is usually soft and sticky. For this reason, it is preferable not to use a mold when preparing this recipe, as removing the chocolate from the mold is bound to be tricky.

Ingredients

12 oz. milk chocolate
¾ cup hazelnut praline (50-60% nuts)

Preparation

1 Melt the chocolate in a bowl as described in step 1 of Melting and Tempering on page 10.

2 Add the hazelnut praline and mix well.

3 Cool the chocolate on the countertop using a spatula and a bench scraper, as described in step 2 of Melting and Tempering on page 10, until the chocolate reaches 75°F.

4 Return chocolate to the bowl and mix well.

5 Once the chocolate mixture is ready, you can use it in one of two ways to create bars:

A Pour and flatten a thin layer of chocolate mixture onto parchment paper, silicone, cellophane or a similar surface. Allow the chocolate mixture to set for 1 hour in a cool room. Break and serve.

B Alternately, pour the chocolate into a chocolate bar mold. Tap the mold against the countertop to release air bubbles between the chocolate and the mold. Remove the excess chocolate from the mold. Allow to set for 2 hours in a cool room. Remove the chocolate bar from the mold and serve.

6 Gianduja Bars may be stored in an airtight container, at room temperature or in the refrigerator for up to 3 months.

CRUSHED COCOA BEAN BARS

Makes

10

sheets

These bars have a dark and earthy flavor sure to delight true chocolate aficionadas!

Ingredients

17½ oz. dark chocolate
½ cup crushed cocoa beans

Preparation

1 Melt the chocolate in a bowl as described in step 1 of Melting and Tempering on page 10, and mix in the cocoa beans.

2 Temper the chocolate mixture, as described in steps 2 and 3 of Melting and Tempering on page 10.

3 Once the chocolate mixture is ready, you can use it in one of two ways to create bars:

A Pour the chocolate into a chocolate mixture bar mold. Tap the mold against the countertop to release air bubbles between the chocolate mixture and the mold. Remove the excess chocolate mixture from the mold. Allow to set for 2 hours in a cool room. Remove the chocolate bar from the mold and serve.

B Alternately, pour a thin layer of chocolate mixture onto cellophane, parchment paper or silicone baking sheet. Allow to set for 1 hour in a cool room. Break and serve.

4 Crushed Cocoa Bean Bars may be stored in an airtight container, at room temperature or in the refrigerator for up to 3 months.

WHITE CHOCOLATE CARAMEL BARS

Makes

5

bars

If you've never tried white chocolate with caramel, now's the time!

Ingredients

1 vanilla bean
17½ oz. white chocolate
½ cup sugar

Preparation

1 Split the vanilla bean in half and scrape the seeds into the white chocolate. Using a double boiler, slowly melt it between 113°F and 118°F.

2 Pour chocolate mixture onto a lightly greased sheet of parchment paper or a 11⅝- x 16 ½-inch silicone-lined baking sheet.

3 In a saucepan, heat the sugar to an amber colored caramel, smoky and bitter. Bubbles will form in the caramel; continue to heat until the bubbles disappear.

4 Very carefully pour the caramel onto another silicone-lined baking sheet or a lightly greased sheet of parchment paper, and immediately flatten using a spatula.

5 Remove the caramel and cut into medium-sized strips. Add the caramel strips to the chocolate mixture.

6 Temper the chocolate mixture, as described in steps 2 and 3 of Melting and Tempering on page 10.

7 Once the chocolate mixture is ready, you can use it in one of two ways to create bars:

   A Pour the chocolate into a chocolate bar mold. Tap the mold against the countertop to remove air bubbles between the chocolate and the mold. Remove the excess chocolate. Allow to set for 2 hours in a cool room. Remove the chocolate bars from the mold and serve.

   B Alternately, pour a thin layer of chocolate mixture onto cellophane, parchment paper or silicone baking sheet. Allow to set for 1 hour in a cool room. Break and serve.

8 White Chocolate Caramel Bars may be stored in an airtight container, at room temperature or in the refrigerator for up to 3 months.

WHITE CHOCOLATE & GREEN TEA BARS

Makes

5

bars

Matcha is a type of green tea used for traditional Japanese tea ceremonies. Combined with white chocolate, the tea's flavor is rich and delicate.

Ingredients

17½ oz. white chocolate

2 tablespoons matcha powder

Preparation

1 Melt the chocolate in a bowl as described in step 1 of Melting and Tempering on page 10.

2 Sprinkle the tea powder over the chocolate and mix well.

3 Temper the chocolate mixture, as described in steps 2 and 3 of Melting and Tempering on page 10.

4 Once the chocolate mixture is ready, you can use it in one of two ways to create bars:

A Pour the chocolate into a chocolate bar mold. Tap the mold against the countertop to release air bubbles between the chocolate and the mold. Remove the excess chocolate from the mold. Allow to set for 2 hours in a cool room. Remove the chocolate bars from the mold and serve.

B Alternately, pour a thin layer of chocolate onto cellophane, parchment paper or a silicone-lined baking sheet. Allow to set for 1 hour in a cool room. Break and serve.

5 White Chocolate & Green Tea Bars may be stored in an airtight container, at room temperature or in the refrigerator for up to 3 months.

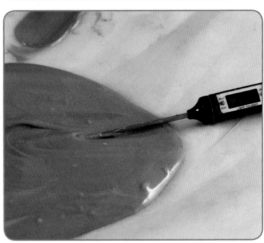

RUM RAISIN & HAZELNUT CHOCOLATE BARS

Makes

5

bars

Just like everyone's favorite raisin and hazelnut bar, but with a KICK of rum!

Ingredients

½ cup dark raisins

2 tablespoons aged dark rum

17½ oz. dark chocolate

½ cup roasted hazelnuts

Preparation

1 Place the raisins in a dish with a lid and pour in the rum.

2 Place the lid on the dish and tilt so that the raisins are covered in rum. Soak overnight in the refrigerator.

3 Melt the chocolate in a bowl as described in step 1 of Melting and Tempering on page 10, and mix in the hazelnuts.

4 Temper the chocolate mixture, as described in steps 2 and 3 of Melting and Tempering on page 10.

5 Separate the raisins from the rum. Add the rum-soaked raisins to the chocolate mixture and mix gently.

6 Once the chocolate mixture is ready, you can use it in one of two ways to create bars:

A Pour the chocolate mixture into a chocolate bar mold. Tap the mold against the countertop to release air bubbles between the chocolate and the mold. Remove the excess chocolate from the mold. Allow to set for 2 hours in a cool room. Remove the chocolate bar from the mold and serve.

B Alternately, pour a thin layer of chocolate onto cellophane, parchment paper or a silicone-lined baking sheet. Allow to set completely for 1 hour in a cool room. Break and serve.

7 Rum Raisin & Hazelnut Chocolate Bars may be stored in an airtight container, at room temperature or in the refrigerator for up to 3 months.

BLACK TEA BARS

Makes

5

bars

This recipe can be prepared using a variety of tea leaves with your favorite type of chocolate. Experiment with tea flavors like Earl Grey, English Breakfast or Orange Pekoe.

Ingredients

17½ oz. dark, milk or white chocolate

3½ tablespoons Earl Grey loose-leaf tea

Preparation

1 Preheat the oven to 100°F.

2 Melt the chocolate in a glass bowl with a lid. Add the tea and close the lid.

3 Place the bowl in the oven and steep overnight.

4 Heat the chocolate mixture to 115°F, then strain with a fine sieve. Apply pressure on the strained tea to extract the last drops of chocolate.

5 Temper the chocolate, as described in steps 2 and 3 of Melting and Tempering on page 10, depending on the type of chocolate used.

6 Once the chocolate mixture is ready, you can use it in one of two ways to create bars:

A Pour the chocolate into a chocolate bar mold. Tap the mold against the countertop to release air bubbles between the chocolate and the mold. Remove the excess chocolate from the mold. Allow to set for 2 hours in a cool room. Remove the chocolate bar from the mold and serve.

B Alternately, pour a thin layer of chocolate onto cellophane, parchment paper or a silicone-lined baking sheet. Allow to set for 1 hour in a cool room. Break and serve.

7 Black Tea Bars may be stored in an airtight container, at room temperature or in the refrigerator for up to 3 months.

MILK CHOCOLATE & SALTED BUTTER BARS

Makes

10

sheets

This smooth and delicious chocolate is best made as sheets which are broken into bars. I don't suggest using a bar mold, as it will be difficult to remove from the chocolate mold.

Ingredients

½ stick (2 oz.) butter
1 tablespoon fine sea salt
1 vanilla bean
17½ oz. milk chocolate

Preparation

1 In a pot, melt the butter over a low heat and add in the salt.

2 Split the vanilla bean and scrape the seeds into the butter. Place the pod in the butter as well.

3 Heat the butter on a low to medium heat for 4-5 minutes, until it gives off a nutty aroma and turns a golden color. Remove from the flame and cool.

4 Melt the chocolate in a bowl as described in step 1 of Melting and Tempering on page 10.

5 Strain the butter into the chocolate and mix.

6 Temper the chocolate mixture, as described in steps 2 and 3 of Melting and Tempering on page 10.

7 Pour the chocolate onto a thin layer onto parchment paper, silicone sheet or cellophane and flatten. Allow to set fully for 1 hour in a cool room. Break into large pieces and serve.

8 Milk Chocolate & Salted Butter Bars may be stored in an airtight container, at room temperature or in the refrigerator for up to 3 months.

PRALINES, TRUFFLES & BONBONS

Belgian-Style (Pralines)

- Rum Raisin Pralines 44
- Gianduja Pralines 46
- Irish Cream Pralines 47
- Whiskey Mousse Pralines 49
- Orange Liqueur Pralines 50
- Raspberry Pralines 52
- Tonka Bean Pralines 53
- Honey & Salt Pralines 55

French-Style (Truffles and Bonbons)

- Champagne or Dark Rum Truffles 56
- Marzipan & Amaretto Mousse Truffles 58
- Milk Chocolate & Rum Truffles 59
- Passion Fruit & Roasted Coconut Truffles 61
- Earl Grey Bonbons 62
- Rocher Bonbons 64
- Marzipan & Ganâche Truffles 65
- Palet d'Or 67

RUM RAISIN PRALINES

Makes about

30

pralines
(One 30-praline mold)

This Rum Raisin Praline is a flavor explosion of dark chocolate, raisins and dark rum! A flavor not to miss!

Ingredients

CHOCOLATE SHELLS
14 oz. dark chocolate (70% cocoa)

FILLING
⅔ cup heavy cream
2 tablespoons corn syrup or glucose
3 tablespoons dark raisins
5 oz. dark chocolate (70% cocoa)
2 tablespoons aged dark rum

Preparation

CHOCOLATE SHELLS

1　Melt and temper the chocolate, as described in Melting and Tempering on page 10.

2　Prepare chocolate shells, as described in Molding and Pralines on page 21.

3　Set aside excess chocolate for assembling the pralines.

FILLING

4　In a saucepan, heat the cream, syrup and raisins. After the mixture reaches a boil, transfer to a tall, narrow dish. Blend with a hand blender, and then strain the mixture.

5　Prepare a ganâche using the cream mixture and chocolate, as described in Ganâche on page 14. When the ganâche is smooth, combine with the rum.

ASSEMBLY

6　Pour the filling into the shells and leave in a cool room to set and dry for a few hours; ideally dry for 24 hours.

7　Melt and temper the chocolate set aside in step 3, as described in Melting and Tempering on page 10. Carefully seal the pralines by drizzling the tempered chocolate over the filled shells in a circular motion from outside to inside. Once the chocolate has partially set, smooth the surface using a scraper. Tap the mold against the countertop to release air bubbles between the chocolate and the mold. Remove excess chocolate from the mold.

8　Allow pralines to cool for 1 hour in a cool room. Remove from mold and serve.

9　Rum Raisin Pralines may be stored in a sealed container in a cool, dark room for up to 2 weeks, or in the refrigerator for 3-4 weeks, however they are best served at room temperature.

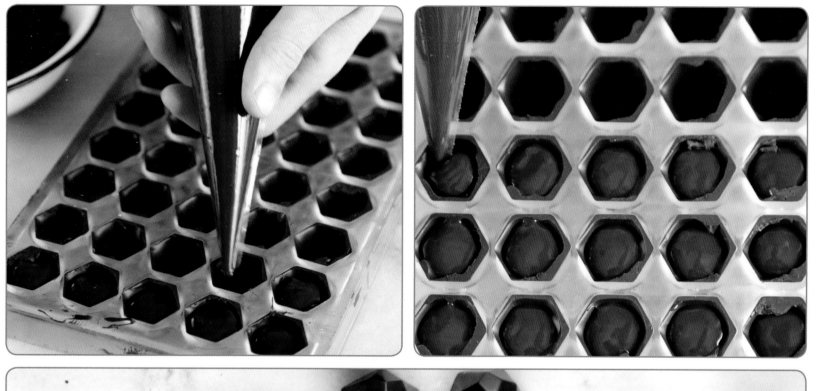

GIANDUJA PRALINES

This recipe is for an unconventional praline, in which the chocolate shells are used as small cups, filled with Gianduja cream. However, these ingredients may also be used to prepare traditional pralines with the cream on the inside.

Makes

30

pralines
(One 30-praline mold)

Ingredients

CHOCOLATE SHELLS
14 oz. dark or milk chocolate

FILLING
For the Dark Chocolate Gianduja
1¾ oz. dark chocolate
1¾ oz. milk chocolate
¾ cup hazelnut praline (50-60% nuts)

For the Milk Chocolate Gianduja
3½ oz. milk chocolate
¾ cup hazelnut praline (50-60% nuts)

Note: For this recipe, choose either dark or milk chocolate for the shells and filling.

Preparation

CHOCOLATE SHELLS
1   Melt and temper the chocolate, as described in Melting and Tempering on page 10 (see note).

2   Prepare the chocolate shells, as described in Molding and Pralines on page 21.

3   Set aside excess chocolate for assembling the pralines.

FILLING
4   In a pot, melt the chocolate of your choice as described in step 1 of Melting and Tempering on page 10, and then add the hazelnut praline.

5   Cool all the mixture on your countertop using a spatula and bench scraper as described in step 2 of Melting and Tempering on page 10, until it reaches 75°F.

6   Transfer to a bowl and mix occasionally, until mixture thickens. The filling should begin to thicken within a few minutes.

ASSEMBLY
7   Pour the filling into a piping tube or pastry bag with a serrated tip. Using a circular motion, fill each chocolate shell with filling. If the filling is runny, wait for 5-10 minutes after piping before continuing to step 8.

8   Melt and temper the chocolate set aside in step 3, as described in Melting and Tempering on page 10. Carefully seal the pralines by drizzling the tempered chocolate over the filled shells in a circular motion from outside to inside. Once the chocolate has partially set, smooth the surface using a scraper. Tap the mold against the countertop to release air bubbles between the chocolate and the mold. Remove excess chocolate from the mold.

9   Allow pralines to cool for 1 hour in a cool room. Remove from mold and serve.

10 Gianduja Pralines may be stored in a sealed container in a cool, dark room for up to 2 weeks, or in the refrigerator for 3-4 weeks, however they are best served at room temperature.

IRISH CREAM PRALINES

Makes

30

pralines
(One 30-praline mold)

Irish Cream is a delight. It's even more delicious with a dose of chocolate.

Ingredients

CHOCOLATE SHELLS
14 oz. white chocolate
2 tablespoons instant coffee

FILLING
2 teaspoons corn syrup or glucose
3 tablespoons espresso
6 oz. white chocolate
¾ oz. milk chocolate
3 tablespoons butter
2 tablespoons whiskey

Preparation

CHOCOLATE SHELLS
1 Melt the chocolate as described in step 1 of Melting and Tempering on page 10. Sift in the instant coffee and mix.

2 Prepare chocolate shells, as described in Molding and Pralines on page 21.

3 Set aside excess chocolate for assembling the pralines.

FILLING
4 Add the syrup to the espresso and mix.

5 Use the coffee mixture, white and milk chocolate, butter and whiskey to prepare a ganâche, as described in Ganâche on page 14.

ASSEMBLY
6 Pour the filling into the shells and leave in a cool room for several hours, ideally 24 hours, to set and dry.

7 Melt and temper the chocolate set aside in step 3, as described in Melting and Tempering on page 10. Carefully seal the pralines by drizzling the tempered chocolate over the filled shells in a circular motion from outside to inside. Once the chocolate has partially set, smooth the surface using a scraper. Tap the mold against the countertop to release air bubbles between the chocolate and the mold. Remove excess chocolate from the mold.

8 Allow pralines to cool for 1 hour in a cool room. Remove from mold and serve.

9 Irish Cream Pralines may be stored in a sealed container in a cool, dark room for up to 2 weeks, or in the refrigerator for 3-4 weeks, however they are best served at room temperature.

WHISKEY MOUSSE PRALINES

Makes

30

pralines
(One 30-praline mold)

Whiskey lovers will swoon over these pralines!

Ingredients

CHOCOLATE SHELLS
14 oz. milk chocolate

FILLING
4 oz. milk chocolate
¼ cup whiskey
¼ cup heavy cream

Preparation

CHOCOLATE SHELLS
1 Melt the milk chocolate as described in step 1 of Melting and Tempering on page 10.

2 Prepare chocolate shells, as described in Molding and Pralines on page 21.

3 Set aside excess chocolate for assembling the pralines.

FILLING
4 Melt the white chocolate as described in step 1 of Melting and Tempering on page 10.

5 Heat the whiskey to 95°F.

6 Prepare a ganâche using the whiskey and chocolate, as described in Ganâche on page 14.

7 In a mixing bowl, whip the cream until fluffy and fold into the ganâche.

8 Pour the ganâche filling into the shells and leave in a cool room for 2 hours to set and dry.

ASSEMBLY
9 Melt and temper the chocolate set aside in step 3, as described in Melting and Tempering on page 10. Carefully seal the pralines by drizzling the tempered chocolate over the filled shells in a circular motion from outside to inside. Once the chocolate has partially set, smooth the surface using a scraper. Tap the mold against the countertop to release air bubbles between the chocolate and the mold. Remove excess chocolate from the mold.

10 Allow to cool and set for 1 hour. Remove the pralines from the mold and place in a sealed container in the freezer. These pralines should be served frozen. Their filling will remain creamy because of the alcohol content.

11 Whiskey Mousse Pralines may be kept in the freezer for 3-4 weeks.

ORANGE LIQUEUR PRALINES

Makes

60

pralines
(Two 30-praline molds)

This praline is made using a slightly complicated technique that creates a liquid, alcohol-based filling. The result of this extra effort will delight your family and friends.

Ingredients

LIQUEUR
Zest of 2 oranges
1 vanilla bean
½ cup whiskey or cognac

CHOCOLATE SHELLS
16 oz. dark chocolate (70% cocoa)

FILLING
1¼ cups sugar
½ cup water

Preparation

LIQUEUR
1   In a bowl, soak the orange zest and vanilla bean in the whiskey for 3-4 hours.

CHOCOLATE SHELLS
2   Melt and temper the chocolate, as described in Melting and Tempering on page 10.

3   Prepare the chocolate shells, as described in Molding and Pralines on page 21. Set aside excess chocolate for assembling the pralines.

FILLING
4   Strain the whiskey into the bowl.

5   In a saucepan, cook the sugar and water together to create syrup. When the syrup reaches 240°F, pour over the whiskey. Pour the mixture back and forth between the bowl and the pot until fully blended (5 or 6 times). Do not use any utensils to mix as they will cause the mixture to separate. Let alcohol syrup cool.

ASSEMBLY
6   When the alcohol syrup has cooled, transfer it to a piping tube or a squeeze bottle. Fill the shells almost to the top. Allow the syrup to set for 24 hours; during this time, the syrup will form a candy crust. This will facilitate the sealing of the pralines.

7   Melt and temper the chocolate set aside in step 3, as described in Melting and Tempering on page 10. Carefully seal the pralines by drizzling the tempered chocolate over the filled shells in a circular motion from outside to inside. Once the chocolate has partially set, smooth the surface using a scraper. Allow the pralines to cool for 1 hour. For a sturdier coating, dip the pralines in chocolate, as described in Dipping and Enrobing on page 18. Remove the pralines from mold and serve.

(continued on page 52)

(continued from page 50)

8 Orange Liqueur Pralines may be stored in a sealed container in a cool, dark room for up to 2 weeks, or in the refrigerator for 3-4 weeks, however they are best served at room temperature.

RASPBERRY PRALINES

Makes

30

pralines
(One 30-praline mold)

These tart treats are an explosion of flavor!

Ingredients

CHOCOLATE SHELLS
11 oz. dark chocolate (70% cocoa)

FILLING
2½ cups seedless raspberry puree (frozen or fresh)
1¾ oz. milk chocolate
1¾ oz. dark chocolate
3½ tablespoons corn syrup or glucose
1¾ oz. butter at room temperature

Preparation

CHOCOLATE SHELLS
1 Melt and temper the chocolate, as described in Melting and Tempering on page 10.

2 Prepare the chocolate shells, as described in Molding and Pralines on page 21.

3 Set aside excess chocolate for assembling the pralines.

FILLING
4 Bring the raspberry puree to a boil.

5 Prepare a ganâche using the raspberry puree, both kinds of chocolate and syrup, as described in Ganâche on page 14. After the ganâche is made, add in the butter.

ASSEMBLY
6 Pour the filling into the shells and leave in a cool room for 24 hours to set and dry.

7 Melt and temper the chocolate set aside in step 3, as described in Melting and Tempering on page 10. Carefully seal the pralines by drizzling the tempered chocolate over the filled shells in a circular motion from outside to inside. Once the chocolate has partially set, smooth the surface using a scraper. Tap the mold against the countertop to release air bubbles between the chocolate and the mold. Remove excess chocolate from the mold. Allow pralines to cool for 1 hour in a cool room. Remove from mold and serve.

8 Raspberry Pralines may be stored in a sealed container in a cool, dark room for up to 1 week, or in the refrigerator for 3-4 weeks, however they are best served at room temperature.

TONKA BEAN PRALINES

Makes

60

pralines
(Two 30-praline molds)

Tonka beans hail from South America. Their powerful flavor is reminiscent of vanilla, almonds, cinnamon and cloves.

Ingredients

CHOCOLATE SHELLS
14 oz. milk chocolate

FILLING
5 tablespoons heavy cream
2 tablespoons corn syrup or glucose
½ Tonka bean, grated
5 oz. milk chocolate
2 tablespoons lightly whipped cream

Preparation

CHOCOLATE SHELLS
1 Melt and temper the chocolate, as described in Melting and Tempering on page 10.

2 Prepare the chocolate shells, as described in Molding and Pralines on page 21.

3 Set aside excess chocolate for assembling the pralines.

FILLING
4 Heat the cream, syrup and grated Tonka bean. Once the mixture has reached a boil, remove from the heat and strain.

5 Prepare a ganâche using the cream mixture and chocolate, as described in Ganâche on page 14.

6 Once the ganâche has reached 95°F to 105°F, fold the lightly whipped cream into the ganâche.

ASSEMBLY
7 Pour the filling into the shells and leave in a cool room for 24 hours to set and dry.

8 Melt and temper the chocolate set aside in step 3, as described in Melting and Tempering on page 10. Carefully seal the pralines by drizzling the tempered chocolate over the filled shells in a circular motion from outside to inside. Once the chocolate has partially set, smooth the surface using a scraper. Tap the mold against the countertop to release air bubbles between the chocolate and the mold. Remove excess chocolate from the mold.

9 Allow pralines to cool for 1 hour in a cool room. Remove from mold and serve.

10 Tonka Bean Pralines may be stored in a sealed container in a cool, dark room for up to 1 week, or in the refrigerator for 3-4 weeks, however they are best served at room temperature.

HONEY & SALT PRALINES

Makes

30

pralines
(One 30-praline mold)

Honey and salt sounds like a strange combination but you'd be surprised
how tasty it can be.

Ingredients

CHOCOLATE SHELLS
14 oz. milk chocolate

FILLING
½ cup heavy cream
2 tablespoons honey
1 vanilla bean, split in half and seeds
scraped

DECORATION
Sea salt or vanilla salt

Preparation

CHOCOLATE SHELLS
1   Melt and temper the chocolate, as described in Melting and Tempering on page 10.

2   Use 8 oz. of the chocolate to prepare the chocolate shells, as described in Molding and Pralines on page 21. Set aside 6 oz. of the chocolate for filling.

3   Set aside excess chocolate for assembling the pralines.

FILLING
4   Heat the cream, honey and vanilla bean together. Steep for 5 minutes, then remove the vanilla bean. Combine with the remaining 6 oz. of tempered chocolate to prepare a ganâche, as described in Ganâche on page 14.

ASSEMBLY
5   Pour the filling into the shells and leave in a cool room for 24 hours to set.

6   Melt and temper the chocolate set aside in step 3, as described in Melting and Tempering on page 10. Carefully seal the pralines by drizzling the tempered chocolate over the filled shells in a circular motion from outside to inside. Once the chocolate has partially set, smooth the surface using a scraper. Tap the mold against the countertop to release air bubbles between the chocolate and the mold. Remove excess chocolate from the mold.

7   Allow pralines to cool for 1 hour in a cool room. Remove from mold, decorate with salt and serve.

8   Honey & Salt Pralines may be stored in a sealed container in a cool, dark room for up to 2 weeks, or in the refrigerator for 3-4 weeks, however they are best served at room temperature.

CHAMPAGNE OR DARK RUM TRUFFLES

60

pralines
(Two 30-praline molds)

A perfect treat for special occasions! Instead of toasting with wine glasses, raise your truffles!

Ingredients

FILLING
¾ cup corn syrup or glucose

¾ cup heavy cream

1½ tablespoons butter

7 oz. dark chocolate (70% cocoa)

3 tablespoons Marc de Champagne or aged dark rum

COATING
25 oz. dark chocolate

¾ cup cocoa powder

Preparation

FILLING
1   Heat the syrup and heavy cream in a saucepan over medium heat, until mixture simmers.

2   Mix the cream mixture, butter and chocolate to prepare a ganâche, as described in Ganâche on page 14. Once the ganâche is smooth, mix in the alcohol.

3   Allow the ganâche to set overnight in a cool room.

4   Lightly beat the ganâche with a handheld whisk for 10-15 seconds, take care not to over whip. The ganâche will solidify within a few minutes.

5   Create grape-sized balls out of the ganâche and allow them to set for several hours.

COATING
6   Melt and temper the chocolate, as described in Melting and Tempering on page 10.

7   Sift the cocoa powder into a wide bowl.

ASSEMBLY
8   Using a dipping fork, dip the chocolate balls in the melted chocolate, as described in Dipping and Enrobing on page 18. Place the truffles in the cocoa powder.

9   Once the chocolate has set, roll the truffles in the cocoa powder.

10 Using a sieve, sift the truffles to remove excess cocoa powder and serve.

11 Champagne or Dark Rum Truffles may be stored in a sealed container in a cool, dark room for up to 1 week, or in the refrigerator for 3-4 weeks, however they are best served at room temperature.

MARZIPAN & AMARETTO MOUSSE TRUFFLES

Makes

100

small truffles
(Four 25-praline molds)

The nutty sweetness of marzipan with milk chocolate is absolutely dreamy!

Ingredients

FILLING
Zest of 2 lemons
1 cup amaretto liqueur
18 oz. marzipan (50% nuts)
⅓ cup cocoa butter

COATING
40 oz. milk chocolate
½ cup powdered sugar

Preparation

FILLING
1 In a small bowl, add the lemon zest to the amaretto at room temperature. Let steep for 15-20 minutes, then strain.

2 Heat the marzipan in a microwave until slightly soft, and then place in a mixer fitted with a paddle attachment.

3 Mix the marzipan on a low speed while slowly dripping in the amaretto mixture, until uniform. Be sure not to add all the amaretto at once, as it will cause the marzipan to clump.

4 Melt the cocoa butter in a pan, and slowly add to the marzipan mixture, keeping the mixer on a low speed.

5 Adjust the mixer to high speed and blend with the wire whip for 10-15 seconds. Allow the mixture to set in the refrigerator for 2 hours, and then at room temperature for 1 hour.

6 Blend the mixture using the wire whip for 2 minutes, or until the color lightens.

7 Using a pastry bag (with or without a tip), pipe ½-inch tubes onto parchment paper. Leave the tubes at room temperature overnight.

8 With a knife, cut the tubes into small marzipan balls about the diameter of a grape, and continue to dry.

COATING
9 Melt and temper the chocolate, as described in Melting and Tempering on page 10.

10 Sift the powdered sugar into a wide bowl.

ASSEMBLY
11 Coat the marzipan bonbons in chocolate, as described in Dipping and Enrobing on page 18.

12 Place the coated marzipan bonbons inside the powdered sugar until they harden. Shake off excess sugar, and serve.

13 Marzipan & Amaretto Mousse Truffles may be stored in a sealed container in a cool, dark room for up to 1 week, or in the refrigerator for 3-4 weeks, however they are best served at room temperature.

MILK CHOCOLATE & RUM TRUFFLES

Makes

These truffles have the bold taste of rum without a strong alcohol aftertaste.

pralines
(Two 30-praline molds)

Ingredients

FILLING
½ cup heavy cream

5 tablespoons corn syrup or glucose

1¾ tablespoons cocoa butter

1 vanilla bean, split in half and seeds scraped

9 oz. milk chocolate

1 stick (4 oz.) butter

3 tablespoons aged dark rum

COATING
25 oz. milk chocolate

Preparation

FILLING
1 Heat the cream, syrup, cocoa butter and vanilla bean and seeds in a saucepan over medium heat, until mixture simmers. Strain.

2 Combine the cream mixture with the chocolate and butter to prepare a ganâche, as described in Ganâche on page 14. Once the ganâche is smooth, add the rum.

3 Allow the ganâche to dry and set overnight in a cool room. Don't mix the ganâche until it is completely stable; otherwise, it will break.

4 Lightly beat the ganâche with a handheld whisk for 10-15 seconds, take care not to over whip. The ganâche will solidify within a few minutes.

5 Roll the ganâche into balls and allow to dry and set for 2-3 hours.

COATING
6 Melt and temper the chocolate, as described in Melting and Tempering on page 10.

ASSEMBLY
7 Use a dipping fork to enrobe the truffles in the chocolate, as described in Dipping and Enrobing on page 18. Allow to cool for 1 hour, then serve.

8 Milk Chocolate & Rum Truffles may be stored in a sealed container in a cool, dark room for up to 1 week, or in the refrigerator for 3-4 weeks, however they are best served at room temperature.

PASSION FRUIT & ROASTED COCONUT TRUFFLES

Makes

70

pralines
(Two 35-praline molds)

These truffles are like a bite-sized vacation.

Ingredients

FILLING
⅔ cup strained, seedless passion fruit puree
17½ oz. white chocolate
1 stick (4 oz.) butter

COATING
1½ cups dessicated coconut
23 oz. white chocolate
70 lollipop sticks or small skewers

Preparation

FILLING
1   Bring the puree to a boil. Combine with the chocolate and butter to create a ganâche, as described in Ganâche on page 14.

2   Leave the ganâche to set in a cool room for a couple of hours, ideally overnight.

3   Roll the mixture into grape-sized balls and place on the tip of a lollipop stick or small skewer. Allow the truffles to dry and set for 4-5 hours.

COATING
4   Roast the coconut in the oven at 300°F, until golden. Place 1 cup of the roasted coconut in a flat dish.

5   Melt the chocolate and mix in the remaining ½ cup of roasted coconut. Temper the mixture, as described in steps 2 and 3 of Melting and Tempering on page 10.

ASSEMBLY
6   Dip the skewered truffles in the chocolate coating and place in the coconut-filled dish. Sprinkle coconut on top of the truffles before the chocolate sets. Once the chocolate has set, shake off excess coconut and serve.

7   Passion Fruit & Roasted Coconut Truffles may be stored in a sealed container in a cool, dark room for up to 1 week, or in the refrigerator for 3-4 weeks, however they are best served at room temperature.

EARL GREY BONBONS

Makes

80

small bonbons

Earl Grey tea is a classic British blend. It has an aromatic taste that is delightful with a bit of dark chocolate.

Ingredients

FILLING
1¾ tablespoons Earl Grey loose-leaf tea
1 cup heavy cream
9½ oz. dark chocolate (70% cocoa)

COATING
21 oz. dark chocolate

Preparation

FILLING

1   Steep the tea in ⅓ cup of heavy cream for 24 hours in the refrigerator.

2   Heat the tea cream to 120°F to release the aroma, and then strain, using a fine sieve. Keep an eye on the heat; don't overheat the tea, as it will evoke bitter flavors.

3   Add the remaining heavy cream to the tea-infused cream.

4   Bring the combined cream to a boil, then blend in the chocolate and prepare a ganâche, as described in Ganâche on page 14.

5   Pour the mixture into a metal frame on a sheet of cellophane, creating an even layer of ¼- to ½-inch deep ganâche. Let set and dry in a cool room for 24 hours.

COATING

6   Melt and temper the coating chocolate, as described in Melting and Tempering on page 10. Cover the ganâche with a small amount of chocolate to create a thin layer of tempered dark chocolate. Set aside the remaining chocolate for dipping. Flip the ganâche over, so that the layer of dark chocolate is now on the bottom.

7   Cut the ganâche into 1-inch cubes. Space cubes apart from one another and allow to set and dry for another 24 hours.

ASSEMBLY

8   Melt and temper again the chocolate set aside for dipping in step 6, as described in Melting and Tempering on page 10.

9   Coat the bonbons in chocolate, as described in Dipping and Enrobing on page 18. Allow to cool for 1 hour and serve.

10 Earl Grey Bonbons may be stored in a sealed container in a cool, dark room for up to 1 week, or in the refrigerator for 3-4 weeks, however they are best served at room temperature.

ROCHER BONBONS

90

bonbons

Rocher is an encrusted chocolate bonbon. Each Rocher is different, depending on the interpretation of the chocolatier who prepares it.
The most famous version is that of Ferrero Rocher, which can be found in supermarkets and candy shops. This is my version.

Ingredients

FILLING
½ cup sugar
½ cup roasted hazelnuts
2½ oz. milk chocolate
2½ oz. dark chocolate (70% cocoa)
1⅓ cups hazelnut praline (50-60% nuts)
⅓ cup crushed wafer rolls

COATING
35 oz. dark chocolate
⅔ cup ground cocoa beans

Preparation

FILLING

1   In a wide pan, heat the sugar to an amber colored caramel.

2   Add the roasted hazelnuts to the sugar, and mix until the nuts are completely covered. Transfer the nuts to a lightly buttered surface.

3   Once the nuts have completely cooled, chop them with a knife or process in a food processor.

4   Melt the chocolates together to 113°F.

5   Add the hazelnut praline and the chopped nuts to the heated chocolate.

6   Stir well and cool the mixture to 75°F. Flatten on parchment paper or cellophane. Cool in the refrigerator for 1 hour.

7   Once the mixture has set slightly, crumble and place in an electric mixer with a paddle attachment. Whip on medium speed for 1-2 minutes, until the color of the mixture lightens.

8   Add in the crushed wafer rolls and gently stir.

9   Roll the mixture into grape-sized balls and leave to set.

COATING

10 Melt the chocolate and cocoa beans together, as described in step 1 of Melting and Tempering on page 10.

ASSEMBLY

11 Using a dipping fork for truffles, dip the balls in the chocolate to create a thin layer as described in step 5 of Dipping and Enrobing on page 18. Allow to cool and serve.

12 Rocher Bonbons may be stored in a sealed container in a cool, dark room for up to 1 week, or in the refrigerator for 3-4 weeks, however they are best served at room temperature.

MARZIPAN & GANÂCHE TRUFFLES

Makes

60

These truffles are almost too pretty to eat.

truffles
(Two 30-praline molds)

Ingredients

FILLING
¾ cup heavy cream
¾ cup corn syrup or glucose
7 oz. dark chocolate (70% cocoa)
2 sticks (8 oz.) butter
5 oz. marzipan

COATING
25 oz. dark chocolate
7 oz. cocoa powder

Preparation

FILLING

1   Heat the cream with syrup in a saucepan over medium heat, until mixture simmers.

2   Prepare a ganâche, using the cream mixture, chocolate and butter, as described in Ganâche on page 14. Allow the ganâche to set overnight in a cool room.

3   Roll the marzipan into small balls. Carefully coat the marzipan balls in ganâche and roll, so that a uniform layer is created. It is best to wear gloves for this step.

4   Allow the balls to dry and set for 2-3 hours.

COATING

5   Melt and temper the chocolate, as described in Melting and Tempering on page 10.

6   Pour the cocoa powder into a wide bowl.

ASSEMBLY

7   Use a dipping fork to dip the balls in the dark chocolate, as described in Dipping and Enrobing on page 18. Rest in the cocoa powder.

8   When the chocolate has hardened, roll the chocolates in the cocoa powder. Place on a sieve to remove excess cocoa and serve.

9   Marzipan & Ganâche Truffles may be stored in a sealed container in a cool, dark room for up to 1 week, or in the refrigerator for 3-4 weeks, however they are best served at room temperature.

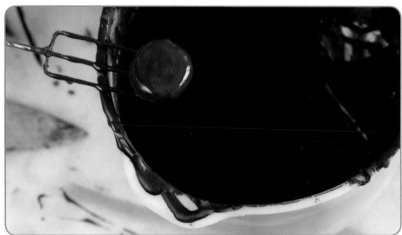
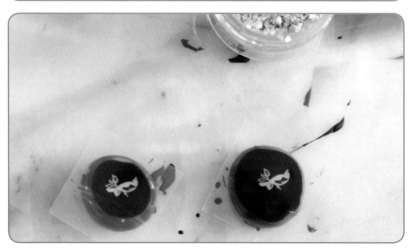

PALET D'OR

Literally meaning "golden disc", the first version of this recipe was made in 1898 by confectioner Bernard Serardy. It was flat and irregularly shaped, with a fragment of gold leaf as decoration.

Ingredients

FILLING
¾ cup heavy cream
1½ tablespoons corn syrup or glucose
7 oz. dark chocolate (70% cocoa)
3 tablespoons butter

COATING
25 oz. dark chocolate (70% cocoa)

DECORATION
Gold leaf (optional)

Preparation

FILLING
1 Heat the cream with syrup in a saucepan over medium heat, until mixture simmers.

2 Mix the cream mixture, chocolate and butter to prepare a ganâche, as described in Ganâche on page 14.

3 Once the ganâche is ready, you can use it in one of two ways to create bonbons:

   A Pour and flatten the ganâche into a cellophane-lined rectangular frame, as described in Dipping and Enrobing on page 18. When set, cut the ganâche into cubes, rectangles or circles (1¼ inches in diameter).

   B Allow the ganâche to set overnight in a cool room. Roll into balls and flatten into discs. Allow the discs to set for an additional day.

COATING
4 Melt and temper the chocolate, as described in Melting and Tempering on page 10.

ASSEMBLY
5 Spread a small amount of chocolate on each disc with your finger and let rest for 1 minute. This will create a stable layer that will simplify the dipping process. Dip the bonbons in chocolate, as described in step 5 of Dipping and Enrobing on page 18.

6 Immediately after dipping, decorate the flat part of each bonbon with gold leaves.

7 Cover top of bonbons with cellophane sheet. Apply with your hand gentle and equal pressure on cellophane to smoothen bonbons. Allow to cool for 1 hour , remove cellophane and serve.

8 Palet d'Or pralines may be stored in a sealed container in a cool, dark room for up to 1 week, or in the refrigerator for 3-4 weeks, however they are best served at room temperature.

CHOCOLATE TREATS

- Chocolate Pencils 71
- Orange & Coffee Batons 72
- Pistachio Ruffles 75
- Christmas Logs 76
- Rice Krispie® Treats 79
- Candied Orange Peels 80
- Candied Pecan Dragées 83
- Pop Rock Dragées 84
- Carmelized Almond Dark Chocolate Dragées 87
- Coffee Bean Dragées 88
- Webbed Chocolate Eggshell 91
- Christmas Trees 92
- Chocolate Toffee 94
- Peanut Snacks 95

CHOCOLATE PENCILS

Makes

10

pencils

Sneak a couple of these treats into your kid's lunch bag on the first day of school.

Ingredients

3½ oz dark, milk or white chocolate
10 thick drinking straws

Preparation

1 Melt and temper the chocolate, as described in Melting and Tempering on page 10.

2 Transfer the chocolate to a piping tube with a small opening.

3 Pipe the chocolate into the straws until they are completely full.

4 Refrigerate for 30 minutes. Remove chocolate from the straws using a skewer.

5 Sharpen one side of the chocolate pencil with a pencil sharpener or knife, and then serve.

6 Chocolate Pencils may be stored in a sealed container for up to 1 year in the refrigerator.

ORANGE & COFFEE BATONS

Makes

30

batons

To make these batons, you will need a sharp plastic card or sheet.

Ingredients

3 oranges
7 oz. dark chocolate (70% cocoa)
⅓ cup ground coffee beans

Preparation

1 Zest the oranges using a fine grater and allow 3-4 hours for the zest to dry.

2 Melt and temper the chocolate, as described in Melting and Tempering on page 10.

3 Pour the chocolate onto plastic wrap that has been stretched over a firm surface. Using a spatula, spread the chocolate to create a rectangle that is ¼ inch deep.

4 Use a plastic card to slice the chocolate into batons. Create a wave shape by undulating the plastic card as you apply pressure into the chocolate.

5 Immediately after cutting the chocolate, sprinkle a fine layer of ground coffee and orange zest over the batons. Cool at room temperature for approximately 20 minutes.

6 Carefully remove the batons from the plastic wrap, and then serve.

7 Orange & Coffee Batons may be stored in a sealed container for up to 1 year in a cool room.

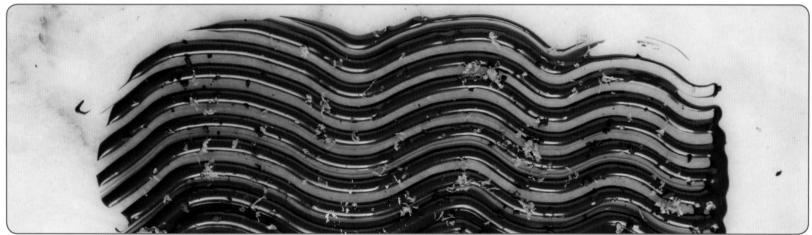

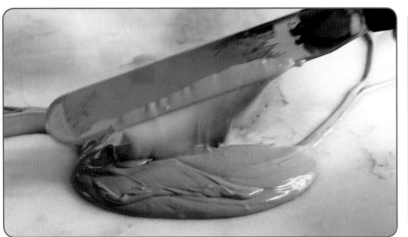

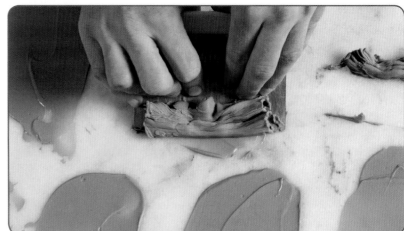
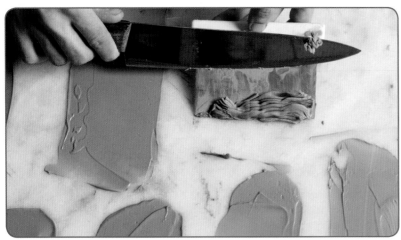

PISTACHIO RUFFLES

Makes

12

bars

This recipe calls for pistachio paste. The best quality paste comes from Italy and has a strong green color.

Ingredients

10½ oz. white chocolate
¼ cup pistachio paste

Preparation

1   Melt the chocolate, as described in step 1 of Melting and Tempering on page 10, and combine with pistachio paste.

2   Transfer the mixture to a countertop. Using a spatula, scrape and stir the chocolate across the countertop, until it reaches 75°F. Return the mixture to a bowl.

3   Spread the chocolate mixture onto the countertop into rectangles, using 2 tablespoons for each one. After 3-4 minutes, use a bench scraper to gather each rectangle into a rippled bar.

4   Allow to cool and set, and then serve.

5   Pistachio Ruffles may be stored in a sealed container for 3-4 weeks in a cool room, or for up to 2 months in the refrigerator.

CHRISTMAS LOGS

Makes

10

logs

These sweet treats are perfect for the festive season!

Ingredients

LOGS
3½ oz. dark chocolate
3½ oz. milk chocolate
¾ cup hazelnut praline (50-60% nuts)
½ cup cocoa powder

COATING
8 oz. dark chocolate

Preparation

LOGS
1. Melt the two types of chocolate together with the hazelnut praline and cocoa powder, as described in step 1 of Melting and Tempering on page 10.

2. Melt and temper the chocolate to 75°F, as described in steps 2 and 3 of Melting and Tempering on page 10.

3. Flatten the mixture between two sheets of baking paper so that a ¾-inch deep sheet is created.

4. Once the chocolate has hardened, cut into ¾-inch wide logs.

COATING
5. Temper the chocolate as described in step 2 and 3 of Melting and Tempering on page 10.

6. Using a silicone brush, paint the logs with one or two coats of chocolate.

7. Allow to cool and set, and then serve.

8. Christmas Logs may be stored in a sealed container for 3-4 weeks in a cool room, or for up to 2 months in the refrigerator.

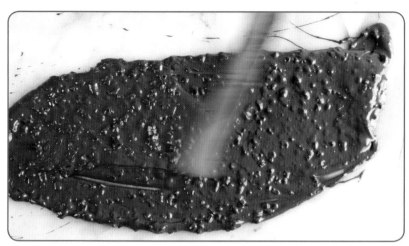

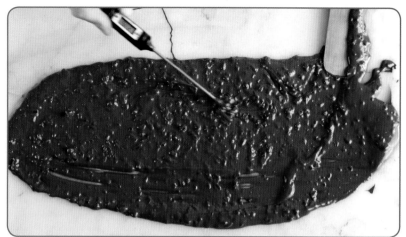

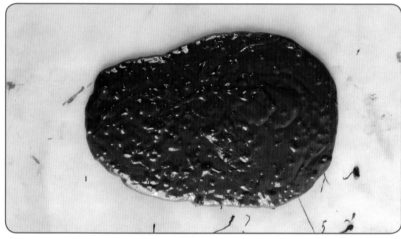

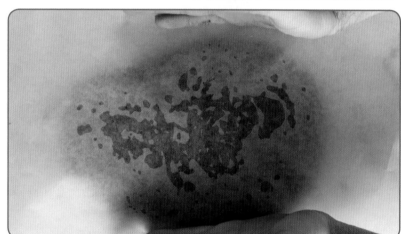

RICE KRISPIE® TREATS

•●■●●■◆●■ ●■■●●■ ●■■◆●■ ●■■◆●■ ●■■●●■◆●■ ●■■◆●■ ●■■◆●■ ●■■◆●■ ●■■◆●■ ●■■◆●■ ●■■

Makes

50

treats

A classic treat upgraded with milk chocolate!

Ingredients

FILLING

5¼ oz. milk chocolate

⅔ cup hazelnut praline

½ teaspoon sea salt

2¼ cups puffed rice (Rice Krispies®)

2¼ cups puffed wheat

COATING

26½ oz. milk chocolate

Preparation

FILLING

1 Melt the chocolate, hazelnut praline and salt, as described in step 1 of Melting and Tempering on page 10. Combine with the puffed rice and puffed wheat. Bring the mixture to 75°F.

2 Pour the mixture onto parchment paper and flatten to create a 1-inch deep rectangle. Allow to cool and set for 20 minutes.

3 Cut into 1- by 1½-inch rectangles and allow to cool at room temperature for an 20 additional minutes, or in the refrigerator for 5 minutes.

COATING

4 Melt and temper the chocolate, as described in Melting and Tempering on page 10.

5 Using a dipping fork, enrobe the treats, as described in Dipping and Enrobing on page 18. Allow to cool and set for 20 minutes, and then serve.

6 Rice Krispie® Treats may be stored in a sealed container in the refrigerator for 3-4 weeks.

CANDIED ORANGE PEELS

Makes

25

skewers

This marriage between orange peels and chocolate is magical.

Ingredients

CITRUS PEELS
2½ cups citrus peels (5-6 lemons, oranges or grapefruits)

1⅓ cups water

3½ tablespoons corn syrup

1 vanilla bean, split in half and seeds scraped

4 cups sugar

25 small Japanese skewers

COATING
20 oz. dark or milk chocolate

Preparation

CITRUS PEELS
1　Slice away the peel from the top and bottom of the fruit.

2　Score the fruit from top to bottom, cutting only into the peel and creating 1½- to 1¾-inch strips. Remove the strips from the body of the fruit.

3　Cook the strips in boiling water for 5 minutes, then pour off the water.

4　Repeat step 3 an additional 3 times, then drain the water completely.

5　Stir together the water, corn syrup, vanilla and seeds and 1 cup of the sugar in a pot. Bring to a simmer. Add the citrus strips and cook over a low flame for 15 minutes.

6　Add 1 cup of the sugar and cook for an additional 15 minutes.

7　Repeat step 6 two more times.

8　After 1 hour of cooking, drain the strips and cool them on a wire rack or parchment paper for 24 hours.

9　Cut the citrus strips into triangles with 1¼- to 1½-inch sides. Place 5 triangles, evenly spaced, on each skewer.

COATING
10　Melt and temper the chocolate in a deep dish, as described in Melting and Tempering on page 10.

ASSEMBLY
11　Dip the skewers in the chocolate and shake well.

12　Place the skewers on cellophane or parchment paper. Alternately, rest the skewers between two dishes so the peels can dry in the air. When the chocolate has set, serve.

13　Candied Orange Peels may be stored in a sealed container in a cool room for 2-3 months.

CANDIED PECAN DRAGÉES

Makes

cup of dragées

Candied pecans can be found at specialty baking stores.
Make them at home instead!

Ingredients

FILLING

½ cup shelled pecans

⅓ cup sugar

2 tablespoons water

COATING

7 oz. milk chocolate

¾ cup hazelnut praline (50-60% nuts)

¼ cup cocoa powder

> Note: You may substitute the filling with ½ cup of store-bought candied pecans.

Preparation

FILLING

1 Roast the pecans in the oven at a low to medium temperature for 7-10 minutes, until golden.

2 In a saucepan, heat the sugar and the water to a clear syrup.

3 Add the roasted pecans to the caramelized sugar and stir well with a wooden spoon or heat-resistant spatula. Once the pecans are completely coated in caramel, transfer them to lightly buttered parchment paper or silicone-lined baking sheet.

4 While the pecans are still hot, separate them from one another, using gloves to prevent burns.

COATING

5 Melt the chocolate, as described in step 1 of Melting and Tempering on page 10, and add the hazelnut praline. Stir the mixture for 3-4 minutes to cool. Transfer to a bowl.

6 Dip the chocolate-covered pecans in the melted chocolate mixture, as described in Dipping and Enrobing on page 18. Once the dragées are fully coated, sprinkle cocoa powder on top. Allow to cool for 10 minutes, and serve.

7 Candied Pecan Dragées may be stored in a sealed container in a cool room for 3-4 weeks.

POP ROCK DRAGÉES

Makes

½

cup of dragées

Get into the kid spirit with these fun candies.

Ingredients

14 oz. milk chocolate

½ cup pop rocks or jumping candies

½ tablespoon edible silver powder, found at specialty candy and baking shops

Preparation

1 Melt and temper the chocolate, as described in Melting and Tempering on page 10.

2 Lay the candies out on a sheet tray and cover them with chocolate, as described in Dipping and Enrobing on page 18. In order to keep the candies separated, add chocolate in small amounts.

3 Once the final coating is complete, allow to dry for 10 minutes. Transfer to a bowl with a lid.

4 Sprinkle the silver powder on top of the mixture and close the lid.

5 Shake the bowl, until the dragées are covered in a fine layer of silver, like small silver nuggets. Serve.

6 Pop Rock Dragées may be stored in a sealed container in a cool room for 3-4 weeks.

CARMELIZED ALMOND DARK CHOCOLATE DRAGÉES

Makes

1

cup of dragées

Make these almond dragées at home for extra freshness and taste!

Ingredients

FILLING
¾ cup whole almonds
⅓ cup sugar
¼ cup water

COATING
7 oz. dark chocolate
7 oz. milk chocolate
¾ cup hazelnut praline (50-60% nuts)
¼ cup cocoa powder

Preparation

FILLING

1 Roast the almonds in the oven on a low to medium heat for 7-10 minutes, until golden.

2 In a pot, heat the sugar and water to make syrup.

3 Add the almonds into the pot and stir with a wooden spoon or heat-resistant spatula. Once all the almonds are completely coated in syrup, transfer to lightly buttered parchment paper or a silicone surface.

4 While the almonds are still hot, separate them from one another, using gloves to prevent burns.

COATING

5 Melt the chocolates together, as described in step 1 of Melting and Tempering on page 10, and combine with the hazelnut praline. Cool the chocolate by moving it around on a countertop, until it reaches 82°F.

6 Transfer the chocolate to a bowl and enrobe the almonds in chocolate, as described in Dipping and Enrobing on page 18.

7 In a separate bowl, sprinkle the cocoa powder over the chocolate-covered almonds and mix well to create a uniform layer of cocoa. Let cool completely and serve.

8 Caramelized Almond Dark Chocolate Dragées may be stored in a sealed container in a cool room for 3-4 weeks.

COFFEE BEAN DRAGÉES

Makes

¾

cup of dragées

Coating the coffee beans shortly after they have been roasted will release their aroma best. These flavors are absorbed by the chocolate and greatly enrich the taste of the dragées.

Ingredients

16 oz. dark chocolate
Zest of 2 lemons
Zest of 2 oranges
⅔ cup coffee beans
3½ tablespoons cocoa powder

Preparation

1   Melt the chocolate, as described in step 1 of Melting and Tempering on page 10, and then mix in the lemon and orange zest.

2   Let the mixture rest for 20 minutes, and then strain with a fine sieve.

3   Melt and temper the chocolate mixture, as described in Melting and Tempering on page 10.

4   In a bowl, add the coffee beans to the chocolate, and mix until all the beans are completely coated in chocolate.

5   While the chocolate is still hot, transfer the beans onto a lightly buttered silicone surface or parchment paper, and separate the beans from each other. Allow the chocolate to cool.

6   Transfer chocolate beans to a clean bowl, sprinkle cocoa powder over the beans and stir gently, until the beans are covered in a fine layer of cocoa powder. Serve.

7   Coffee Bean Dragées may be stored in a sealed container in a cool room for 3-4 weeks.

  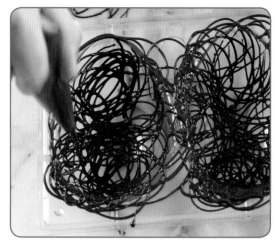

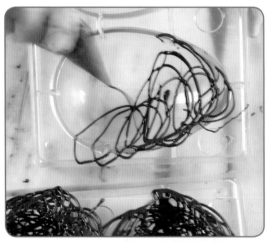  

WEBBED CHOCOLATE EGG SHELL

Makes

1

egg
(with a 6-8 inch egg-shaped chocolate mold)

Show off your skills with this treat!

Ingredients

7 oz. dark, milk or white chocolate

Preparation

1 Melt and temper the chocolate, as described in Melting and Tempering on page 10.

2 Transfer the chocolate into a plastic bag or disposable piping tube, and cut the tip to create a small hole.

3 Make circular movements while piping the chocolate into both sides of the mold. Be sure to cover most of the surface area of the egg mold, creating a web effect.

4 Once the chocolate has hardened, scrape away the excess chocolate from the edges of the mold. Allow to set for 1 hour in a cool room or for 15 minutes in the refrigerator.

5 Carefully remove the chocolate halves from the mold and heat the edges of the eggs on a warm platter or stovetop. Place the two halves together. Allow to set for 15 minutes, and serve.

6 Webbed Chocolate Eggshell may be stored in the refrigerator for up to 1 week.

CHRISTMAS TREES

● ■ ●

Makes

12

trees

Make a day of sprucing up both your real Christmas tree and these small ones. The decoration for this recipe may be replaced with store-bought chocolate balls in a variety of colors, and without alcohol.

Ingredients

Decoration

RED BALLS

1 oz. white chocolate

2 teaspoons cocoa butter

1 pinch red powdered food dye

3 tablespoons chocolate pearls

METALLIC BALLS

3-4 drops vodka

3 tablespoons chocolate pearls

1 pinch gold powdered food dye

1 pinch silver powdered food dye

TREES

1½ cups marzipan

2 tablespoons pistachio puree

COATING

18 oz. dark chocolate

DECORATING

⅓ cup ground pistachios

Preparation

RED BALLS

1 Melt the white chocolate, as described in step 1 of Melting and Tempering on page 10. Add the cocoa butter and red dye.

2 In a bowl, drip the white chocolate mixture over the chocolate pearls. Mix until the pearls are completely enrobed in white chocolate.

3 Repeat step 2 until the chocolate pearls are coated evenly.

METALLIC BALLS

4 In a bowl, drip the vodka over the chocolate pearls and mix well.

5 Sprinkle the gold and silver food dye over the pearls, and mix until the pearls are completely enrobed.

TREES

6 Mix together the marzipan and pistachio puree. Flatten the mixture between 2 sheets of parchment paper to create a ⅜-inch deep sheet.

7 Remove the parchment paper and cut out trees using a tree-shaped cookie cutter.

COATING

8 Melt and temper the chocolate, as described in Melting and Tempering on page 10.

9 Use a silicone brush to create a thin layer of chocolate on one side of each marzipan tree. Dry for 10 minutes.

10 Using a dipping fork, enrobe the trees in chocolate, as described in Dipping and Enrobing on page 18.

(continued on page 94)

(continued from page 92)

DECORATING

11 After dipping, adorn the trees with the colored chocolate balls, sprinkle with a pinch of ground pistachios, and serve.

12 Christmas Trees may be stored in a sealed container in the refrigerator for 3-4 weeks.

CHOCOLATE TOFFEE

Makes

80-100

pieces

This ooey-gooey treat is a classic!

Ingredients

4 teaspoons sugar syrup (using equal parts sugar and water)

1 cup sugar

3 tablespoons water

1 cup heavy cream

Pinch of salt

1 vanilla bean, split and seeds scraped

6 oz. dark chocolate or 10 oz. milk chocolate

1½ tablespoons butter

Preparation

1 Heat the syrup with sugar in a saucepan over medium heat for 4-5 minutes, to make a caramel. Stir with a heat-resistant spatula to create a smooth texture. Pour the water into the caramel and combine.

2 Heat the heavy cream in a separate pot over medium heat for 4-5 minutes. Add the cream to the caramel and mix.

3 Add the salt and vanilla bean and seeds to the caramel mixture, and heat to 240°F. Remove the vanilla bean, add in the chocolate and mix well.

4 Add butter and mix well.

5 Cover and cool for 2 days at room temperature.

6 Roll the toffee into balls and wrap with candy wrappers or a piece of thin cellophane cut into squares.

7 Chocolate Toffee may be stored in a sealed container for up to 1 month in a cool room, or for 2 months in the refrigerator.

PEANUT SNACKS

Makes

10-12

snacks

Getting ready to watch the World Series at home? These snacks bring the ballpark into your living room.

Ingredients

PEANUT SNACKS
¾ cup roasted, salted peanuts
5¼ oz. milk chocolate
½ cup peanut butter

COATING
10 oz. milk chocolate

Preparation

PEANUT SNACKS
1   Chop the peanuts with a sharp knife or food processor.

2   Melt the chocolate, as described in step 1 of Melting and Tempering on page 10. Combine with the peanut butter and chopped peanuts.

3   Cool the peanut mixture by spreading and folding it on a countertop. Once the mixture has cooled to between 78°F-82°F, transfer it onto a sheet of cellophane and allow it to harden.

COATING
4   Once the peanut mixture has set, melt and temper the chocolate, as described in Melting and Tempering on page 10.

5   Place the peanut mixture, smooth side up, on the countertop, and coat in a thin layer of chocolate. Allow to cool and set for 20 minutes.

6   Flip the peanut mixture over, so that the chocolate is on the bottom. Cut into 2-inch by 1-inch sticks. Using a dipping fork, enrobe the sticks in the remaining chocolate, as described in Dipping and Enrobing on page 18. Allow to cool before serving.

7   Peanut Snacks may be stored in a sealed container for 3-4 weeks, or for 2 months in the refrigerator.

CHOCOLATE DESSERTS

- Chocolate Ice Cream 98
- Gianduja Parfait 101
- Frozen Chocolate Cream with Jagermeister 102
- Chocolat Soufflé 104
- Milk Chocolate Caramel Ice Cream 105
- Cookies 'n' Cream Popsicles 107
- Chocolate Eclairs 108
- Chocolate Crème Chantilly 109
- Mille Feuilles Speculus Cookies 110
- White Chocolate Espresso Sorbet 112
- Hot Chocolate with Marshmallows 114
- Chocolate Crème Brûlée 115
- Valentine's Day Fondue 117
- Panna Cotta with Streusel Topping 118

CHOCOLATE ICE CREAM

Makes

2½ to 3

cups of ice cream

Chocolate ice cream is a classic favorite of kids and adults alike. Surprise your family with a chocolate sundae for dessert!

Ingredients

1 vanilla bean, split in half and seeds scraped
1 cup milk
2 egg yolks
½ cup plus 3 tablespoons sugar
3 tablespoons milk chocolate
3 tablespoons cocoa powder
⅔ cup heavy cream

Preparation

1   In a pot, bring the vanilla bean and seeds and milk to a simmer.

2   In a clean bowl, beat the egg yolks and sugar.

3   Remove the vanilla bean, pour the milk into the egg yolks and beat well.

4   Return the mixture to the pot and heat to 175°F.

5   In a bowl, melt the milk chocolate as described in step 1 of Melting and Tempering on page 10. Add the chocolate and cocoa powder to the vanilla mixture and mix with an immersion blender.

6   Add the cream and continue to blend.

7   Refrigerate for at least 4 hours.

8   Blend the mixture again and strain.

9   Chill in an ice cream maker and serve.

10 Chocolate Ice Cream may be stored in an airtight container in the freezer for 3-4 weeks.

GIANDUJA PARFAIT

Makes

10

servings

Attention nut lovers, this one's for you!

Ingredients

ALMOND CRUMBLE

½ stick (2 oz.) butter

¾ cup plus 2 tablespoons powdered sugar

⅓ cup almond powder

¾ cup plus 2 tablespoons flour

PARFAIT

1 cup hazelnut or walnut paste (50-60% nuts)

3½ oz. milk chocolate

3 tablespoons butter

⅓ cup water

½ cup sugar

2 egg whites

1½ cups heavy cream

HAZELNUT RUM CREAM

¼ cup heavy cream

¾ cup plus 2 tablespoons hazelnut praline (50-60% nuts)

¼ cup aged dark rum

Preparation

ALMOND CRUMBLE

1   Preheat oven to 325°F. Using an electric mixer with a paddle attachment, soften the butter with the powdered sugar.

2   Add in the almond powder and flour, and continue to mix until walnut-sized pieces form.

3   Spread the crumble onto a parchment paper or a silicone-lined baking sheet and bake at 325°F for 12 minutes, or until golden.

PARFAIT

4   Place the hazelnut praline, milk chocolate and butter in a bowl. Heat in the microwave for 1 to 2 minutes, until the butter has melted, and mix together.

5   Heat the water with ¼ cup of sugar to create a syrup.

6   At the same time, in a separate bowl or stand mixer, beat the egg whites with the remaining sugar.

7   When you see bubbles in the syrup and the egg whites are stable, pour the syrup onto the egg whites, and continue to beat for several minutes until cool.

8   Fold a third of the egg white mixture into the chocolate mixture and blend well.

9   Gently fold the remaining egg white mixture into the chocolate.

10   Whip the cream until it is firm and light.

11   Fold the cream into the chocolate until smooth.

12   Pour into a rectangular pan or a silicone dish, and freeze for at least 3 hours.

(continued on page 102)

(continued from page 101)

HAZELNUT RUM CREAM

13 Heat the cream to 95°F. Slowly add the cream into the hazelnut praline and mix.

14 Add the rum and mix well.

ASSEMBLY

15 Cover a plate with a layer of crumble, and remove parfait from freezer.

16 Release the parfait from its dish by heating the sides of the dish with hot towels or a hair dryer. Cut the parfait into rectangles. Rest the parfait rectangles on top of the crumble.

17 Spoon out a dollop of hazelnut rum cream next to the parfait and serve.

18 The individual elements of the recipe may be stored in airtight containers in the refrigerator for up to 1 week.

FROZEN CHOCOLATE CREAM WITH JAGERMEISTER

Makes

6-8

shot glasses

Jagermeister is a German digestif made of 56 different herbs and spices. In this recipe, Jagermeister may be substituted with Amaretto, whiskey, cognac, Triple Sec, Limoncello, Campari or vodka.

Ingredients

3½ oz. dark chocolate (70% cocoa)
½ cup heavy cream
½ cup Jagermeister

Preparation

1 Prepare a ganâche using the chocolate and ¼ cup of the cream, as described in Ganâche on page 14.

2 Add the Jagermeister and mix well.

3 Whip the remaining ¼ cup of cream to a high froth.

4 Fold the cream into the ganâche completely, until smooth.

5 Transfer the mixture to a disposable pastry bag and fill the shot glasses.

6 Freeze for several hours, and then serve.

7 Frozen Chocolate Cream with Jagermeister may be stored in an airtight container in the freezer for 3-4 weeks.

Frozen Chocolate Cream with Jagermeister

CHOCOLATE SOUFFLÉ

Makes

6-8

ramekins
(2½- to 3-inch)

Soufflé may sound complicated but it is actually quick and easy to prepare.

Ingredients

½ stick (2 oz.) butter
⅓ cup + ½ cup sugar
1⅓ cups milk
2 teaspoons flour
2 teaspoons cornstarch
10½ oz. dark chocolate (70% cocoa)
6 egg whites
3 egg yolks

Preparation

1   Generously butter the ramekins. Fill the ramekins with ⅓ cup sugar, move around all the sides, and then remove the excess, so that the inside of each ramekin is coated in a layer of sugar.

2   Refrigerate the ramekins.

3   Mix the milk, flour and cornstarch into a smooth batter.

4   Bring the batter to a boil while stirring.

5   Remove the batter from the heat and mix in the chocolate. Mix well until the chocolate is fully melted.

6   In a mixing bowl, beat the egg whites, while slowly adding in ½ cup sugar, until the mixture is light and fluffy.

7   Mix one-third of the egg mixture into the chocolate batter, and then fold in the egg yolks. Blend well and fold in the remaining egg whites.

8   Fill the ramekins to three-quarters full.

9   Refrigerate for at least 2-3 hours.

10 Preheat the oven to 350°F.

11 Bake for 7–8 minutes. Serve immediately.

12 Unbaked Chocolate Soufflé may be stored in an airtight container in the refrigerator for 3-4 days.

MILK CHOCOLATE CARAMEL ICE CREAM

Makes

2½ to 3

cups of ice cream

Milk chocolate and caramel make an unbeatable pair. Waffle cones really help to bring out the flavor of this ice cream.

Ingredients

½ cup sugar

⅔ cup water

1 vanilla bean, split in half and seeds scraped

⅔ cup milk

2 egg yolks

5 oz. milk chocolate

⅔ cup heavy cream

Preparation

1 Heat the sugar in a saucepan over medium heat for 2-3 minutes, until it thickens and turns a caramel color.

2 Slowly drip water into the caramel, and stir.

3 Add the vanilla bean and seeds and milk to the mixture. Bring to a simmer.

4 In a clean bowl, beat the egg yolks.

5 Pour the caramel mixture into the egg yolks and whisk.

6 Return the mixture to the pot and heat to 175°F. Remove vanilla bean.

7 Transfer the mixture to a bowl. Add in chocolate and combine with an immersion blender.

8 Pour in the heavy cream and continue to blend.

9 Refrigerate for at least 4 hours.

10 Blend again and strain. Chill in an ice cream maker for 20-25 minutes and serve.

11 Milk Chocolate Caramel Ice Cream may be stored in an airtight container in the freezer for 3-4 weeks.

COOKIES 'N' CREAM POPSICLES

Makes

10

popsicles

This recipe combines ice cream with cookies. As an alternative, you may leave the cookie unbaked, creating cookie-dough ice cream. The cookies may also be substituted with other toppings, like almonds and walnuts. Dark chocolate ice cream is delicious with a ground cocoa topping.

Ingredients

BUTTER COOKIES
½ stick (2 oz.) butter

⅓ cup water

1 egg yolk

¾ cup plus 2 tablespoons flour

1 pinch of salt

POPSICLES
Frozen dark or milk chocolate ice cream with caramel (see Chocolate Ice Cream on page 98 or Milk Chocolate Caramel Ice Cream on page 105)

10 popsicle sticks

COATING
Dark Chocolate Coating
21 oz. dark chocolate (70% cocoa)

⅓ cup grape seed oil or canola oil

Milk Chocolate Coating
21 oz. milk chocolate

⅓ cup grape seed oil or canola oil

Preparation

BUTTER COOKIES
1   Preheat oven to 300F.

2   In a bowl, mix butter, water, egg yolk, flour and salt, until mixture is uniform.

3   Transfer mixture to refrigerator and cool for 1 hour.

4   Remove from refrigerator. Using a rolling pin, flatten between 2 sheets of parchment paper to create a ⅛-inch sheet.

5   Bake for 10-12 minutes, until completely golden.

6   Cool and crumble into big pieces.

POPSICLES
7   Mix two-thirds of the cookie crumbles into the ice cream.

8   Using a popsicle mold or similar dish, fill the molds with the ice cream, and then place the popsicle sticks deep into each popsicle mold. Freeze for 3-4 hours until completely firm.

COATING
9   Melt the chocolate, either dark or milk, as described in step 1 of Melting and Tempering on page 10, and transfer to a narrow, deep bowl. Add in the oil and the rest of the cookie crumbles.

10 Dip the popsicles in the chocolate and cool and set in the freezer.

11 Cookies 'n' Cream Popsicles may be stored in an airtight container in the freezer for 3-4 weeks.

CHOCOLATE ÉCLAIRS

14

éclairs

Bring the bakeries of Paris into your kitchen with these delectable treats!

Ingredients

ÉCLAIRS
1 cup milk
1 teaspoon salt
1 stick (4 oz.) butter
⅔ cup flour
5 eggs

FILLING
1 cup heavy cream
1 cup milk
5 egg yolks
¼ cup sugar
8 oz. dark chocolate (70% cocoa)

COATING
¾ cup heavy cream
⅓ cup sugar syrup
5 oz. dark chocolate (70% cocoa)

Preparation

ÉCLAIRS

1 Preheat the oven to 475°F.

2 In a pot, heat the milk, salt and butter.

3 Add in the flour and stir with a wooden spoon, until the batter solidifies.

4 Transfer the batter to an electric mixer with a paddle attachment, and mix for 2-3 minutes.

5 Add the eggs, one at a time, and continue to mix. It may not be necessary to add all five eggs to achieve a soft and smooth texture. If the required consistency is achieved after adding only 4 eggs, don't add the fifth one.

6 Transfer the batter to a piping tube fitted with a round ¾-inch tip. Pipe ½-inch long tubes onto parchment paper or a silicone-lined baking dish.

7 Bake for 2-3 minutes until golden. Lower the temperature of the oven to 350°F and continue to bake for an additional 12 minutes. Do not open the oven while baking. Remove from oven and cool.

FILLING

8 In a small saucepan, heat the heavy cream and milk on low to medium heat.

9 In a mixing bowl, whip the egg yolks and sugar.

10 When the milk mixture is hot, add the egg yolks to it, while stirring.

11 Continue to heat the mixture for 4-5 minutes, until it froths and thickens.

12 Strain the mixture. Prepare a ganâche, using the egg and milk mixture and the chocolate, as described in Ganâche on page 14. Chill in an airtight container for 4 hours.

COATING

13 Heat the heavy cream with syrup in a saucepan over medium heat, until mixture simmers.

14 Prepare a ganâche, using the mixture and the dark chocolate, as described in Ganâche on page 14.

ASSEMBLY

15 Transfer the chocolate cream filling to a piping tube with a ¼-inch tip.

16 Hold one of the éclairs in the palm of your hand, with the side that touched the baking sheet facing up. Stick the tip in close to the edge and pipe in the filling just until the éclair feels substantially heavier. Repeat with the other éclairs.

17 Transfer the warm chocolate into a bowl. Lightly dip the top side of the éclair in the chocolate mixture. Repeat with the other éclairs. Allow to cool for 2-3 minutes and serve.

18 Chocolate Éclairs may be stored in an airtight container in the refrigerator for 3 days.

CHOCOLATE CRÈME CHANTILLY

Makes

6-8

servings

Chocolate Pencils (page 71) are a wonderful companion for this recipe.

Ingredients

⅔ cup milk

10½ oz. dark chocolate (70% cocoa)

1½ cups heavy cream

2 tablespoons aged dark rum (optional)

Preparation

1 In a small saucepan, warm the milk on medium heat until it simmers. Use the milk and chocolate to prepare a Ganâche, as described on page 14.

2 Whip the heavy cream until it is fluffy.

3 When the ganâche has cooled to 95°F, fold in the whipped cream. If desired, add in rum.

4 Allow the mixture to set for 3-6 hours, and then transfer into cups or bowls.

5 Chocolate Crème Chantilly may be stored in an airtight container the refrigerator for 3-4 days.

MILLE FEUILLES SPECULUS COOKIES

Makes

30

cookies

Mille Feuilles means 1,000 layers, and these cookies are as beautiful as they are delicious.

Ingredients

GANÂCHE
10½ oz. milk chocolate
⅔ cup heavy cream

CRÈME CHANTILLY
1 cup heavy cream

SPECULUS COOKIES
1 dash of salt
Zest of 1 lemon
½ teaspoon baking powder
1 stick (4 oz.) butter
½ cup Muscovado sugar
⅓ cup brown sugar or molasses
1 egg yolk
2 cups flour

Preparation

GANÂCHE
1   Prepare a ganâche, using the milk chocolate and heavy cream, as described in Ganâche on page 14.

2   Separate 1 cup of the ganâche for use with the crème chantilly. Cover and refrigerate the remainder.

CRÈME CHANTILLY
3   Whip the heavy cream until fluffy.

4   When the ganâche is between 95°F-115°F, fold 1 cup of the ganâche in cream. Cover and refrigerate for 2-3 hours.

SPECULUS COOKIES
5   Place the salt, lemon zest, baking powder, butter, Muscovado and brown sugar in an electric mixer fitted with a paddle attachment.

6   Mix for 2 minutes until the butter is soft, and then add the egg yolk. Continue to mix for 1 minute.

7   Add in the flour and mix until the ingredients blend together. The brown sugar should crystallize.

8   Knead the dough and flatten between 2 sheets of parchment paper into a very thin rectangle.

9   Remove the top sheet of parchment paper. With a knife and ruler, or a square cookie cutter, cut the dough into 1½-inch squares. There is no need to space the squares apart after cutting.

10 Allow the squares to rest, while preheating the oven to 325°F for 20 minutes.

(continued on page 112)

(continued from page 110)

11 Bake the dough for 12 minutes until golden. If necessary, cut the cookie squares to separate them. Refrigerate in an airtight dish.

ASSEMBLY

12 Each cookie is made of 3 layers. The first layer contains a dollop of ganâche between the 1st and 2nd speculus squares. The second layer contains a dollop of crème chantilly between the 2nd and 3rd speculus squares.

13 **First layer:** With a piping tube fitted with a round tip, pipe a small amount of ganâche between two squares.

14 **Second layer:** With a clean piping tube, pipe a dollop of crème chantilly on top. Rest a final square on top.

15 Serve immediately.

16 Mille Feuilles Speculus Cookies may be stored in an airtight container in the refrigerator for 3-4 days.

WHITE CHOCOLATE ESPRESSO SORBET

Makes

2 to 2½

cups of sorbet

This sorbet is delicious as a topping for coffee cake or on its own.

Ingredients

7 (1½ cups) espresso shots
1½ tablespoons corn syrup or glucose
3½ oz. white chocolate

DECORATION
Coffee beans

Preparation

1 Combine the espresso and syrup and blend well.

2 Prepare a ganâche with the coffee mixture and white chocolate, as described in Ganâche on page 14.

3 Refrigerate ganâche for 1 hour.

4 Chill in an ice cream maker according to the manufacturer's instructions. Decorate with coffee beans and serve.

5 White Chocolate Espresso Sorbet may be stored in an airtight container in the freezer for 3-4 weeks.

White Chocolate Espresso Sorbet

HOT CHOCOLATE WITH MARSHMALLOWS

Makes

6 to 8

cups

This recipe is great for kids or anyone who wants to feel like a kid again!
This chocolate drink can also be served cold, so it can be adapted to fit any season!

Ingredients

MARSHMALLOWS
2 tablespoons gelatin powder
½ cup water
1 cup sugar
1 vanilla bean, split in half and seeds scraped
¾ cup honey
¼ cup powdered sugar

HOT CHOCOLATE
1 quart milk
2 teaspoons honey
2 cinnamon sticks
6 oz. dark chocolate (70% cocoa)
2½ oz. milk chocolate

Preparation

MARSHMALLOWS
1 Soak gelatin powder in ¼ cup of water for 5 minutes, and then heat in the microwave for 1 minute.

2 In a saucepan, heat the sugar, remaining ¼ cup of water and vanilla bean and seeds to 240°F.

3 Place the honey in an electric mixer. Add the gelatin and sugar syrup, and whip on medium speed for 8 minutes.

4 Pour out honey mixture and flatten on a lightly greased surface and allow to set for 8 hours.

5 Using lightly greased scissors, cut the marshmallow in cubes.

6 Sprinkle the cubes with powdered sugar. Marshmallows may be stored in an airtight container for 3-4 weeks.

HOT CHOCOLATE
7 Heat the milk, honey and cinnamon sticks in a saucepan over medium heat, until mixture simmers.

8 Melt both types of chocolate in a bowl, as described in step 1 of Melting and Tempering on page 10.

9 Strain the milk mixture, slowly pour it over the chocolate and mix well. Reserve 1 cup of milk mixture in the pot.

10 Transfer the chocolate mixture to the saucepan with the remaining milk mixture and let simmer for 3 minutes. Hot chocolate mixture may be stored in an airtight container in the refrigerator for up to 1 week.

ASSEMBLY
11 Pour the hot chocolate into mugs or cups. Garnish with the marshmallow cubes and serve immediately.

CHOCOLATE CRÈME BRÛLÉE

Makes

6

servings

Preparing the perfect crème brûlée is a challenge for any chef. It's a great way to earn your gourmand spurs.

Ingredients

1½ cups heavy cream

1 cup milk

1 vanilla bean

5 egg yolks

⅓ cup sugar

7 oz. dark chocolate (70% cocoa), or 7 oz. white chocolate, or 6⅓ oz. milk chocolate

½ cup white sugar or Muscovado sugar

Preparation

1 Preheat the oven to 250°F.

2 Pour the cream and milk into a saucepan.

3 Split and scrape the vanilla bean into the saucepan.

4 Heat over a low flame.

5 In a clean bowl, beat together the egg yolks and sugar.

6 Once the milk mixture is hot, whisk it into the egg yolks.

7 Melt the chocolate in a separate bowl, as described in step 1 of Melting and Tempering on page 10.

8 Strain the milk and egg yolk mixture.

9 Pour a small amount of the egg yolk mixture into the chocolate, and mix well.

10 Repeat step 9, slowly adding more of the egg mixture until it is completely blended into the chocolate.

11 Pour the mixture into small ramekins, and place them in a large pan filled with warm water—the water should reach the line of the custard.

12 Bake ramekins for 30 minutes. Remove ramekins from oven and allow to cool.

13 Wrap each ramekin in plastic wrap and refrigerate for 12 hours.

14 Before serving, sprinkle a small amount of Muscovado sugar on top of the custard, and caramelize using a kitchen blowtorch. Alternately, with the oven on a top grill setting, heat the sugar-coated custards for 2-3 minutes.

15 Before adding the sugar layer, the Chocolate Crème Brûlée may be stored, covered in cellophane, in the refrigerator for 3-4 days.

VALENTINE'S DAY FONDUE

Makes

10

servings

This recipe provides two variations of chocolate fondue: dark chocolate fondue and white chocolate hazelnut fondue. The preparation process for both variations is very similar.

Ingredients

DARK CHOCOLATE FONDUE
⅓ cup milk
⅓ cup heavy cream
1 vanilla bean, split in half and seeds scraped
⅓ cup sugar syrup or corn syrup
13 oz. dark chocolate (70% cocoa)

WHITE CHOCOLATE HAZELNUT FONDUE
⅓ cup milk
⅓ cup heavy cream
1 vanilla bean, split in half and seeds scraped
15 oz. white chocolate
¾ cup hazelnut praline (50-60% nuts)

RECOMMENDED DIPPING FRUITS
½ lb. red, seedless grapes
½ pineapple, sliced
4 peeled kiwis

Preparation

1 In a pot, heat the milk, heavy cream, vanilla bean and seeds and sugar syrup (if making Dark Chocolate Fondue).

2 Using a double boiler or microwave, melt the chocolate as described in step 1 of Melting and Tempering on page 10. For the White Chocolate Hazelnut Fondue, add the hazelnut praline and mix well.

3 Strain the milk mixture. Prepare a ganâche, using the mixture and the chocolate, as described in Ganâche on page 14.

4 Serve the fondue warm with chopped fruit for dipping. Fondue may be stored in an airtight container in the refrigerator for 2-3 days.

PANNA COTTA WITH STREUSEL TOPPING

Makes

8

servings

Panna Cotta is an Italian classic, and simple to make at home with this easy recipe.

Ingredients

PANNA COTTA
2½ teaspoons gelatin powder
1 cup milk
1 cup heavy cream
⅓ cup sugar
4½ oz. dark chocolate (70% cocoa)

STREUSEL
2⅓ tablespoons butter
2⅓ tablespoons powdered sugar
2⅓ tablespoons almond flour
1¾ tablespoons flour
1 pinch of salt

CHOCOLATE SAUCE
¼ cup milk
1⅓ tablespoons corn syrup
1½ oz. dark chocolate (70% cocoa)

Preparation

PANNA COTTA

1 Soak the gelatin powder in ¼ cup of milk.

2 Heat the remaining ¾ cup of milk with the heavy cream and sugar to 95°F.

3 Prepare a ganâche, using the milk mixture, the gelatin mixture and the dark chocolate, as described in Ganâche on page 14.

4 Pour panna cotta into 8 serving bowls and refrigerate for 1 hour.

STREUSEL

5 Preheat the oven to 325°F.

6 Cut the butter into cubes and place in a bowl.

7 Sift together the powdered sugar, both types of flour and salt and add to the butter. Knead the mixture until it is crumbly.

8 Bake the dough on parchment paper or a silicone-lined baking sheet for 10-12 minutes. Remove from oven and allow to cool for 20 minutes.

CHOCOLATE SAUCE

9 Heat the milk and corn syrup together. Prepare a ganâche, using the milk mixture and the dark chocolate, as described in Ganâche on page 14.

ASSEMBLY

10 Sprinkle 1 tablespoon of streusel on top of each serving of panna cotta. Garnish with a dollop of sauce.

11 Each of the Panna Cotta with Streusel Topping 3 elements may be stored separately in airtight containers in the refrigerator for up to 1 week.

CHOCOLATE COOKIES & CAKES

- Chocolate Tart 123
- Brownies 124
- Black Current & Chocolate Mousse Cake 127
- Salted Butter Tart 128
- Chocolate Parmesan Biscuits 130
- Chocolate Lava Cakes 133
- Chocolate Chip Cookies 134
- Valentine's Day Macaron Hearts 137
- Chocolate Marzipan Sponge Cake 138
- Blondies 141

CHOCOLATE TART

Makes **8** servings

A simple and elegant dessert for the sophisticated palate.

Ingredients

CAKE BASE
1 stick (4 oz.) butter
½ teaspoon salt
⅓ cup powdered sugar
1 egg
3 tablespoons almond flour
1¾ tablespoons cocoa powder
¾ cup flour

FILLING
½ cup almond flour
½ cup sifted powdered sugar
4 eggs
¼ cup heavy cream
2 teaspoons corn flour
2 tablespoons cocoa powder
¼ teaspoon baking powder
2½ oz. dark chocolate

GANÂCHE
¾ cup heavy cream
7 oz. dark chocolate (70% cocoa)
¼ cup corn syrup

GARNISH
2½ oz. dark chocolate (70% cocoa)

Preparation

CAKE BASE
1 Using an electric mixer fitted with a wire whisk attachment, blend the butter, salt and powdered sugar until they are fully mixed.

2 Add the egg, almond flour and cocoa powder, and continue to mix until smooth.

3 Add the flour gradually and continue to mix, until the batter is uniform.

4 Preheat the oven to 325°F.

5 Flatten the batter between 2 sheets of parchment paper to create a 12-inch circle. Remove the top sheet of parchment paper and transfer sheet with the dough onto the baking pan. Place in the refrigerator for 30 minutes.

6 Using a fork, poke small holes into the dough.

7 Bake for 8 minutes. Remove from the oven and cool. Lower oven temperature to 300°F.

FILLING
8 Blend together all of the ingredients, except for the chocolate oven.

9 Melt the chocolate, as described in step 1 of Melting and Tempering on page 10, and blend into the mixture. Pour the mixture into the baked crust and bake at 300°F for 12 minutes. Remove from the oven and cool.

GANÂCHE
10 Use all of the ingredients to prepare a ganâche, as described in Ganâche on page 14.

11 Once the tart has cooled, fill the top with the ganâche. Set aside to cool.

(continued on page 124)

(continued from page 123)

GARNISH

12 Melt and temper the chocolate, as described in Melting and Tempering on page 10.

13 Using a rolling pin, flatten the chocolate between 2 sheets of cellophane to create a thin sheet. Cool in the refrigerator for 15 minutes.

14 Remove the cellophane from the chocolate. Holding a metal spatula with the blade side down at a 45° angle to the sheet, press firmly into the chocolate, pushing steadily forward until a curl forms in the chocolate. Repeat to create enough chocolate curls to cover the top of the cake. Carefully lift the curls with a toothpick or a small skewer, place on the tart and serve.

15 Chocolate Tart may be wrapped and stored in the refrigerator for up to 1 week.

BROWNIES

Makes

16

brownies

No dessert fills your home with a smell as delightful as the aroma of freshly baked brownies. Beware! You may need to find a good hiding place for them because these brownies are simply irresistible.

Ingredients

½ cup almonds
½ cup hazelnuts
3½ oz. dark chocolate (70% cocoa)
1 stick (4 oz.) butter
2 tablespoons vegetable oil
3 eggs
¾ cup golden sugar
⅓ cup flour

Requires an 8-inch by 12-inch baking pan

Preparation

1 Preheat the oven to 350°F.

2 Roast the almonds and hazelnuts in the oven for 7 to 10 minutes, until golden. Allow the nuts to cool slightly.

3 Chop the nuts with a knife or in a food processor.

4 In a saucepan, gently melt together the chocolate, butter and oil.

5 Using an electric mixer, beat the eggs while slowly adding in the sugar, until the mixture is light and fluffy.

6 Fold ⅓ of the egg mixture into the chocolate.

7 Transfer the chocolate mixture into the egg mixture, and fold together.

8 Fold in the flour and nuts.

9 Pour the batter into a lightly-buttered baking pan and bake for 15 minutes. Allow the brownies to cool and set before serving.

10 Brownies may be stored in an airtight container at room temperature for 1 week.

Brownies

BLACK CURRANT & CHOCOLATE MOUSSE CAKE

Makes
8-10
servings

This cake is the grown-up version of an ice-cream cake. It's perfect for a warm summer night!

Ingredients

CAKE BASE
3 large eggs
⅓ cup sugar or honey
⅓ cup heavy cream
3½ oz. dark chocolate (70% cocoa)
2 tablespoons cocoa powder
2½ tablespoons flour

BLACK CURRANT MOUSSE
⅓ cup black currant puree
9 oz. white chocolate
½ cup heavy cream

DARK CHOCOLATE MOUSSE
⅔ cup milk
10½ oz. dark chocolate (70% cocoa)
¾ cup heavy cream

Requires a 9-inch by 12-inch baking pan and a round 10-inch baking pan

Preparation

CAKE BASE
1. Preheat the oven to 325°F. Lightly grease a 9- by 12-inch baking pan.

2. In a mixing bowl, beat the eggs and sugar together for 4-5 minutes, until the mixture is light and fluffy.

3. In a small pot, bring the heavy cream to a boil, and then pour it onto the chocolate. Mix until the chocolate is fully melted. If the chocolate does not melt, reheat the mixture in the microwave for 10-15 seconds.

4. Fold the chocolate cream into the egg mixture.

5. Sift the cocoa powder and flour into the batter.

6. Pour the batter into the baking pan and bake for 12 minutes. Remove the cake from the oven. Allow to cool. The cake should be moist after baking, as it will harden after cooling.

7. Place the cake, while still in the pan, in the freezer.

BLACK CURRANT MOUSSE
8. Heat the black currant puree and white chocolate together until fully melted, as described in step 1 of Melting and Tempering on page 10.

9. In a separate bowl, whip the heavy cream for 2-3 minutes until it doubles in volume.

10. Cool the black currant mixture to around 95°F, then mix in the whipped cream. Remove the cake base from the freezer. Immediately pour the black currant mixture onto the frozen cake base and return it to the freezer for 2-3 hours.

11. When the cake and the mousse are completely frozen, remove the cake from the freezer and cut away the edges. Remove the cake from the pan. Clean the pan and replace the cake in the cleaned baking pan. Return cake to freezer.

(continued on page 128)

(continued from page 127)

DARK CHOCOLATE MOUSSE

12 In a small pot, bring the milk to a boil, and then pour a third of the boiling milk onto the dark chocolate.

13 Once the chocolate has fully melted, gradually pour in the rest of the milk. Stir until the cream is smooth and shiny.

14 In a separate bowl, whip the heavy cream for 2-3 minutes, until it doubles in volume.

15 Cool the chocolate cream to around 95°F and mix in the whipped cream.

ASSEMBLY

16 Remove cake from freezer. Pour the dark chocolate mousse onto the frozen black currant mousse and cool in the refrigerator for 2-3 hours.

17 Remove the cake by slightly heating the base of the pan, and serve.

18 Black Currant & Chocolate Mousse Cake may be wrapped and stored in the refrigerator for 4-5 days.

SALTED BUTTER TART

Makes

8-10

servings

The combination of salty and sweet is a true winner!
This tart is both creamy and light on the tongue.

Ingredients

CAKE BASE

1 stick (4 oz.) butter

½ teaspoon salt

⅓ cup powdered sugar

1 egg

2¾ tablespoons almond flour

¾ cup flour

Preparation

CAKE BASE

1 Preheat the oven to 325°F. Lightly grease a tart pan.

2 Using an electric mixer with a wire whisk attachment, whip the butter, salt and powdered sugar

3 Add the egg and almond flour.

4 Add a third of the flour, and continue to mix for 2-3 minutes until smooth.

5 Add the remaining flour and mix for 1 additional minute.

6 Flatten the dough between 2 sheets of parchment paper to create a 12-inch circle.

FILLING

½ cup sugar

¼ cup water

1 stick (4 oz.) butter

2 eggs

1 egg yolk

½ cup flour

1 pinch of salt

½ teaspoon baking powder

COATING

¾ cup heavy cream

Seeds from 1 vanilla bean

1 teaspoon sea salt

9 oz. milk chocolate

½ cup sugar

⅓ cup water

GARNISH (OPTIONAL)

3 oz. white chocolate

Requires a round 10-inch tart pan

7   Remove the top sheet of the parchment paper and transfer the batter, facing down, to the tart pan. When the dough is in the pan, remove the second sheet of parchment paper.

8   Refrigerate for 30 minutes. Use a fork to puncture small holes in the dough.

9   Bake for 8 minutes. Remove cake base from oven and allow to cool. Do not turn oven off.

FILLING

10   In a saucepan, heat ¼ cup of sugar over medium heat for 3-4 minutes, until golden. Add the water and stir until smooth.

11   Remove the caramel syrup from the heat and add butter. Transfer the mixture to a mixing bowl.

12   Add the eggs, egg yolk and remaining ¼ cup of sugar, and mix well.

13   Sift in the flour, salt and baking powder. Mix for 2-3 minutes until smooth.

14   Pour into the tart base and bake for 12-14 minutes.

COATING

15   Prepare a ganâche using the heavy cream, vanilla seeds, sea salt and chocolate, as described in Ganâche on page 14.

16   In a saucepan, heat the sugar over medium heat for 3-4 minutes, until golden. Add water and stir until smooth.

17   Mix the syrup with the ganâche. The mixture should be between 95°F and 105°F.

18   Pour over the tart and cool for 20 minutes.

GARNISH (OPTIONAL)

19   Melt and temper the white chocolate, as described in Melting and Tempering on page 10.

20   Flatten the chocolate between 2 sheets of cellophane to create a thin sheet of chocolate.

21   Roll the chocolate, still wrapped in cellophane, into a spiral and refrigerate for 15 minutes.

22   Unroll the chocolate, attempting not to break the sheet. Carefully place on top of the tart and serve.

23   Salted Butter Tart may be wrapped and stored in the refrigerator for up to 1 week.

CHOCOLATE PARMESAN BISCUITS

Makes
35
cookies

For those whose sweet tooth is less prominent, these biscuits make a great snack.

Ingredients

COOKIES
⅓ cup grated Parmesan cheese
1 stick (4 oz.) butter
1 egg yolk
2 teaspoons milk
1 teaspoon ground cayenne pepper
½ cup flour

COATING
7 oz. milk chocolate

Preparation

COOKIES
1   Preheat the oven to 325°F.

2   In a mixing bowl, mix the cheese and butter together.

3   Add the egg yolk, milk and pepper, and mix.

4   Add the flour and mix well.

5   Transfer the batter to a piping bag and pipe out small rectangles onto a parchment paper-lined sheet tray.

6   Bake for 10-12 minutes. Remove from the oven and cool on a wire rack for 20 minutes.

COATING
7   Melt and temper the chocolate, as described in Melting and Tempering on page 10.

8   Using your fingers, enrobe half of each cookie in chocolate. Place on cellophane or parchment paper and allow the cookies to set for 10 minutes. Serve.

9   Chocolate Parmesan Biscuits may be stored in an airtight container in a cool room for 2-3 weeks.

CHOCOLATE LAVA CAKES

Makes

8

servings

With its hot fudge center and crumbly exterior, this cake is an explosion of chocolate. If it's cold outside, this cake will certainly warm your guests. Chocolate Ice Cream (see page 98) makes an excellent topping.

Ingredients

GANÂCHE
½ cup milk
2 tablespoons glucose or corn syrup
4 oz. dark chocolate (70% cocoa)

CAKE BATTER
8 oz. dark chocolate (70% cocoa)
½ cup marzipan
1 dash of salt
1 cup heavy cream
6 eggs
⅓ cup sugar
⅓ cup flour

Requires 8 round 3-inch by 3-inch cake rings and 8 small, disposable plastic cups

Preparation

GANÂCHE

1 Prepare a ganâche with the milk, sugar syrup and dark chocolate, as described in Ganâche on page 14.

2 Pour into small disposable cups (1 inch less in diameter than cake rings), spaced slightly apart from each other.

3 Freeze for 1½ hours.

CAKE BATTER

4 Preheat the oven to 325°F.

5 In a mixing bowl, melt the chocolate, marzipan and salt, while stirring.

6 In a pot, bring the cream to a boil. Slowly mix the cream into the chocolate mixture.

7 In a separate bowl, whip the eggs and sugar for 4 minutes until the mixture is fluffy.

8 Fold the eggs into the chocolate mixture.

9 Sift in the flour and mix until smooth.

ASSEMBLY

10 Line the rings with strips of parchment paper that have been buttered on both sides. Alternately, use buttered disposable baking pans of a similar size.

11 Fill two-thirds of each ring with cake batter.

12 Remove the frozen ganâche from the disposable cups and place in the center of the batter, without letting it touch the bottom of the ring. Cover with more batter.

13 Bake for 15 minutes.

(continued on page 134)

(continued from page 133)

14 Let cakes cool for 10 minutes. Remove baking rings and parchment paper. To make this process easier, freeze the cakes while still in the baking rings, and remove once frozen. Reheat before serving. Serve hot or warm.

15 Chocolate Lava Cakes may be stored in an airtight container in the refrigerator for 3-4 days.

CHOCOLATE CHIP COOKIES

Makes **35** cookies

Milk and cookies can improve even the toughest day. This quick and easy recipe makes the dreamiest cookies.

Ingredients

1 stick (4 oz.) butter
⅔ cup brown or Muscovado sugar
1 egg
¾ cup flour
¾ teaspoon baking powder
1 dash of sea salt
2½ oz. dark chocolate (65-75% cocoa)
⅔ cup chocolate chips or chocolate pearls
⅔ cup chopped walnuts

Preparation

1 Preheat the oven to 325°F.

2 In a mixing bowl, using an electric mixer with a paddle attachment, mix the butter and sugar together until creamy.

3 Add the egg and continue to mix.

4 Add in the flour, baking powder and salt, and continue to mix until smooth.

5 In a saucepan, melt the dark chocolate as described in step 1 of Melting and Tempering in page 10, and add into the batter.

6 Add in the chocolate chips and walnuts. Continue to mix.

7 Refrigerate the batter for 20 minutes.

8 Remove batter from refrigerator and flatten it between two sheets of parchment paper. Using a cookie cutter or small knife, cut out 2-inch diameter cookies.

9 Bake on a parchment paper or silicone-lined baking sheet for 10-12 minutes.

10 Cool on a wire rack.

11 Chocolate Chip Cookies may be stored in an airtight container at room temperature for 1 week.

Chocolate Chip Cookies

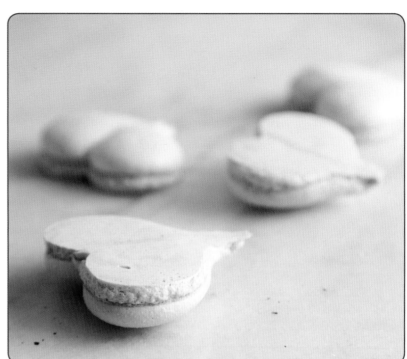

VALENTINE'S DAY MACARON HEARTS

Makes

18

large macarons

Instead of buying a Valentine's Day present, surprise your special someone with these very special treats.

Ingredients

MACARONS

1¼ cups almond flour

1½ cups powdered sugar

½ cup egg whites

¾ cup granulated sugar

¼ cup water

3-4 drops red food coloring

FILLING

9 oz. white chocolate

½ cup strained raspberry puree

3-4 drops rose water

¾ cup heavy cream

Preparation

MACARONS

1   Preheat the oven to 275°F.

2   In a food processor, mix the almond flour and powdered sugar. Sift together.

3   Add half of the egg whites to the flour mixture and mix well.

4   In an electric mixer, whisk together the remaining egg whites with ¼ cup of the granulated sugar. Whip the sugar and egg white mixture for 2-3 minutes on a high speed to create a soft meringue.

5   In the meantime, in a pot, bring the remaining granulated sugar and water to a boil.

6   Once the syrup reaches 225°F, slowly pour into the meringue, while continuing to whip. Add in 3-4 drops of food coloring and continue to mix for 8 minutes.

7   Fold the meringue into the flour mixture until it is smooth. Transfer mixture to a piping tube fitted with a ¾-inch tip. To create a heart shape on parchment paper, pipe out a circle, 1¼ to 1½-inches in diameter. Use a spoon to spread the batter upwards and to the right. Pipe out another circle of the same size, close to the first one. Spread the batter upwards and to the left. Fashion the bottom tip of the heart with the spoon. The two circles will now be in the shape of a heart. Pipe the remaining batter and allow the hearts to dry for 20 minutes.

8   Transfer the parchment paper to a baking sheet and bake for 14-16 minutes. Remove from the oven and allow baked hearts to cool completely before removing from the parchment paper.

FILLING

9   Melt the chocolate, as described in step 1 of Melting and Tempering on page 10. Use

(continued on page 138)

(continued from page 137)

the melted chocolate and raspberry puree to prepare a ganâche, as described in Ganâche on page 14. Add rose water and mix.

10 Whip the heavy cream until it is fluffy. Fold the cream into the ganâche when it reaches 95°F and refrigerate for 3-4 hours.

ASSEMBLY

11 Transfer the chilled filling to a piping tube.

12 Match the hearts in pairs according to size.

13 Pipe out a small amount of filling onto the flat side of 1 heart. Carefully place the flat side of the second heart onto the filling.

14 Refrigerate for 24 hours before serving.

15 Valentine Day's Macaron Hearts may be stored in an airtight container in the refrigerator for up to 1 week.

CHOCOLATE MARZIPAN SPONGE CAKE

Makes

16

servings

This fluffy cake goes great with coffee.

Ingredients

CAKE BASE (OPTIONAL)
1½ cups marzipan

CAKE
½ oz. butter for greasing
4 eggs
½ cup sugar or honey
½ cup heavy cream
4½ oz. dark chocolate (70% cocoa)

Preparation

CAKE BASE (OPTIONAL)
1 Flatten the marzipan between 2 sheets of parchment paper to create an 8- by 12-inch sheet.

2 Remove the parchment paper and transfer the marzipan to the bottom of the cake pan.

CAKE
3 Preheat the oven to 325°F. Lightly grease the cake pan.

4 In a mixing bowl, whip the eggs and sugar (or honey) for 5 minutes, until the mixture is fluffy.

(continued on page 140)

Chocolate Marzipan Sponge Cake

(continued from page 138)

½ cup marzipan
1⅓ tablespoons cocoa powder
¼ cup flour
3-4 drops orange blossom essence

COATING
1½ cups heavy cream
4½ oz. dark chocolate (70% cocoa)

CHOCOLATE SHEET
9 oz. dark chocolate (70% cocoa)

Requires a rectangular 8-inch by 12-inch cake pan

5 In a pot, bring the heavy cream to a boil. In a separate mixing bowl, pour the cream over the dark chocolate. Mix well.

6 In a separate mixing bowl, pour the chocolate cream onto the marzipan, and mix well.

7 Fold a quarter of the egg mixture into the marzipan cream, and mix well. Fold the remaining egg mixture into the marzipan cream.

8 Sift the cocoa powder and flour into the mixture, and mix. Add the orange blossom essence.

9 Pour the batter into the cake pan and bake for 20 minutes. Cool on a wire rack for 10 minutes.

10 Freeze the cake, still in cake pan, for 2 hours.

11 Remove the cake from the pan and cut in half (along the length) to create 2 long cakes. Cut the cakes into two rectangles, each ¾ inches wide.

COATING
12 Prepare a ganâche, using ½ cup of the heavy cream and the chocolate, as described in Ganâche on page 14.

13 Mix in the remaining cream and refrigerate for at least 4 hours.

14 Whip the ganâche until it is fluffy, making sure not to over mix.

CHOCOLATE SHEET
15 Melt and temper the chocolate, as described in Melting and Tempering on page 10.

16 Using a rolling pin, flatten the chocolate between 2 pieces of cellophane to create a thin sheet. Refrigerate for 20 minutes.

17 Remove the cellophane from chocolate sheet and break into shards.

ASSEMBLY
18 Transfer the coating to a piping tube with a ¼-inch tip.

19 Pipe a dollop of coating on each cake rectangle and garnish with several shards of the chocolate sheet.

20 Chocolate Marzipan Sponge Cake may be stored in an airtight container in the refrigerator for 2-3 days.

BLONDIES

Makes

16

blondies

Blondies are a fun alternative to regular chocolate brownies—they tend to be a bit lighter on the tongue.

Ingredients

½ cup almonds

½ cup hazelnuts

1 stick (4 oz.) butter

2 tablespoons vegetable oil

7 oz. white chocolate

3 eggs

⅔ cup Muscovado sugar

⅓ cup flour

Requires an 8-inch by 12-inch baking pan

Preparation

1   Preheat the oven to 350°F.

2   Roast the almonds and hazelnuts in the oven for 7 to 10 minutes, until golden. Allow the nuts to cool slightly.

3   Chop the nuts with a knife or in a food processor.

4   In a pot, heat the butter on a low to medium heat, until golden.

5   Remove butter from heat. Mix in the oil and chocolate, until the entire mixture is melted.

6   Using an electric mixer, beat the eggs while slowly adding in the sugar, until the mixture is light and fluffy.

7   Fold ⅓ of the egg mixture into the chocolate.

8   Transfer the chocolate into the remaining egg mixture, and fold together.

9   Fold in flour and roasted nuts.

10   Pour the batter into a lightly-buttered baking pan, and bake for 15 minutes. Allow the blondies to cool and set before serving.

11   Blondies may be stored in an airtight container at room temperature for 1 week.

METRIC EQUIVALENTS

The recipes that appear in this cookbook use the standard United States method for measuring liquid and dry or solid ingredients (teaspoons, tablespoons and cups). The information on this chart is provided to help cooks outside the U.S. successfully use these recipes. All equivalents are approximate.

METRIC EQUIVALENTS FOR DIFFERENT TYPES OF INGREDIENTS

A standard cup measure of a dry or solid ingredient will vary in weight depending on the type of ingredient. A standard cup of liquid is the same volume for any type of liquid. Use the following chart when converting standard cup measures to grams (weight) or milliliters (volume).

Standard Cup	Fine Powder (ex. flour)	Grain (ex. rice)	Granular (ex. sugar)	Liquid Solids (ex. butter)	Liquid (ex. milk)
1	140 g	150 g	190 g	200 g	240 ml
¾	105 g	113 g	143 g	150 g	180 ml
⅔	93 g	100 g	125 g	133 g	160 ml
½	70 g	75 g	95 g	100 g	120 ml
⅓	47 g	50 g	63 g	67 g	80 ml
¼	35 g	38 g	48 g	50 g	60 ml
⅛	18 g	19 g	24 g	25 g	30 ml

USEFUL EQUIVALENTS FOR DRY INGREDIENTS BY WEIGHT

(To convert ounces to grams, multiply the number of ounces by 30.)

1 oz	=	¹⁄₁₆ lb	=	30 g
4 oz	=	¼ lb	=	120 g
8 oz	=	½ lb	=	240 g
12 oz	=	¾ lb	=	360 g
16 oz	=	1 lb	=	480 g

USEFUL EQUIVALENTS FOR LENGTH

(To convert inches to centimeters, multiply the number of inches by 2.5.)

1 in				=	2.5 cm			
6 in	=	½ ft		=	15 cm			
12 in	=	1 ft		=	30 cm			
36 in	=	3 ft	=	1 yd	=	90 cm		
40 in				=	100 cm	=	1 m	

USEFUL EQUIVALENTS FOR DRY INGREDIENTS BY WEIGHT

¼ tsp						=	1 ml	
½ tsp						=	2 ml	
1 tsp						=	5 ml	
3 tsp	=	1 tbls			½ fl oz	=	15 ml	
		2 tbls	=	⅛ cup	=	1 fl oz	=	30 ml
		4 tbls	=	¼ cup	=	2 fl oz	=	60 ml
		5 ⅓ tbls	=	⅓ cup	=	3 fl oz	=	80 ml
		8 tbls	=	½ cup	=	4 fl oz	=	120 ml
		10 ⅔ tbls	=	⅔ cup	=	5 fl oz	=	160 ml
		12 tbls	=	¾ cup	=	6 fl oz	=	180 ml
		16 tbls	=	1 cup	=	8 fl oz	=	240 ml
		1 pt	=	2 cups	=	16 fl oz	=	480 ml
		1 qt	=	4 cups	=	32 fl oz	=	960 ml
					=	33 fl oz	=	1000 ml = 1 liter

USEFUL EQUIVALENTS FOR COOKING/OVEN TEMPERATURES

	Fahrenheit	Celsius	Gas Mark
Freeze Water	32° F	0° C	
Room Temperature	68° F	20° C	
Boil Water	212° F	100° C	
Bake	325° F	160° C	3
	350° F	180° C	4
	375° F	190° C	5
	400° F	200° C	6
	425° F	220° C	7
	450° F	230° C	8
Broil			Grill

INDEX

A - B

Almond Dragées, 17

Black Tea Bars, 39

Black Current & Chocolate Mousse Cake, 127

Blondies, 141

Brownies, 124

C

Candied Orange Peels, 80

Candied Pecan Dragées, 83

Caramelized Almond Dark Chocolate Dragées, 87

Champagne or Dark Rum Truffles, 56

Chocolate Chip Cookies, 134

Chocolate Crème Brûlée, 115

Chocolate Crème Chantilly, 109

Chocolate Doll, 25

Chocolate Eclairs, 108

Chocolate Ice Cream, 98

Chocolate Lava Cakes, 133

Chocolate Marzipan Sponge Cake, 138

Chocolate Parmesan Biscuits, 130

Chocolate Pencils, 71

Chocolate Soufflé, 104

Chocolate Tart, 123

Chocolate Toffee, 94

Christmas Logs, 76

Christmas Trees, 92

Coffee Bean Dragées, 88

Cookies 'n' Cream Popsicles, 107

Cream-Filled Chocolate Shells, 23

Crushed Cocoa Bean Bars, 32

E - F - G

Early Grey Bonbons, 62

Frozen Chocolate Cream with Jagermeister, 102

Ganâche-Filled Bonbons, 18

Gianduja Bars, 31

Gianduji Parfait, 101

Gianduja Pralines, 46

H - I

Honey & Salt Pralines, 55

Hot Chocolate with Marshmallows, 114

Irish Cream Pralines, 47

M

Marzipan & Amaretto Mousse Truffles, 58

Marzipan & Ganâche Truffles, 65

Milk Chocolate & Nougat Bars, 30

Milk Chocolate & Rum Truffles, 59

Milk Chocolate & Salted Butter Bars, 41

Mille Feuilles Speculus Cookies, 110

Milk Chocolate Caramel Ice Cream, 105

O - P

Orange & Coffee Batons, 72

Orange Liqueur Pralines, 50

Palet d'Or, 67

Panna Cotta with Streusel Topping, 118

Passion Fruit & Roasted Coconut Truffles, 61

Peanut Snacks, 95

Peppermint Chocolate Bars, 29

Pistachio Ruffles, 75

Pop Rock Dragées, 84

R

Raspberry Pralines, 52

Rice Krispie® Treats, 79

Rocher Bonbons, 64

Rum Raisin & Hazelnut Chocolate Bars, 38

Rum Raisin Pralines, 44

S - V

Salted Butter Tart, 128

Tonka Bean Pralines, 53

Valentine's Day Fondue, 117

Valentine's Day Macaroon Hearts, 137

W

Webbed Chocolate Egg Shell, 91

Whiskey Mousse Pralines, 49

White Chocolate & Green Tea Bars, 36

White Chocolate Caramel Bars, 35

White Chocolate Espresso Sorbet, 112